SANCTUARY

in TIME

A SABBATH RETREAT GUIDEBOOK

SANCTUARY *in* TIME

A SABBATH RETREAT GUIDEBOOK

BY CHUCK CERVENKA

XULON PRESS

Xulon Press
2301 Lucien Way #415
Maitland, FL 32751
407.339.4217
www.xulonpress.com

Printed in the United States of America.

ISBN-13: 978-1-54565-590-0

Endorsements:

"A Sanctuary in Time was exactly what I needed to renew my soul and refresh my walk with the Lord. I serve a small congregation in the Indianapolis area as Senior Pastor. After much rearranging in my schedule I was finally able to get away for a Spiritual Retreat. I took nothing with me but my Bible and my journal. On a table at the retreat center was Sanctuary in Time: A Sabbath Retreat Guidebook. I loved it and found it just right for this season and my time in retreat. I am a trained Spiritual Director and have read many resources but have not found such a clear guidebook in any of my readings. Thank you so much for your investment and heart for healthy soul care."

In God's Grace – Reverend Arlene Weigand

"Sabbath is a necessity created as a gift by God for us, often overlooked because of the world's demands. It is all too common for guests of Be Still Retreats to not know where to start when it comes to intentionally planning true sabbath rest. Sanctuary in Time is a beautifully written tool that brings the reader to the correct posture to truly have fresh, focused fellowship with God. We have seen the testimony of joy found in sabbath rest with God over and over. Thank you, Chuck, for making this book available to our guests."

For His glory,
Jesse and Lindsay Urban,
Founders of Be Still, Inc.

"After reading For God's Sake, Rest! and attending one of our Sabbath Retreats. Chuck Cervenka took a group of men on a Sabbath retreat for several days in the Smoky Mountains in Tennessee. Since that first retreat, he has published a practical guide for such retreats. I am indebted to Chuck for making my contribution more applicable through a step by step daily progression."

Jim Anderson, Author of For God's Sake Rest

"What started as a trail blazed by Pastor Cervenka's journey towards the rest promised in Hebrews 4:11 has since become a well-worn path as other disciples have found the rewards of both the journey and the destination of this trail. I heartily recommend this book as a guide to the rarely-enjoyed but indescribably beneficial discipline of Sabbath"

Reverend David E. Thomas
Pastor of Flint Hills Community Church
Cottonwood Falls, KS

To my wife Karen,
who watched, waited, and prayed for me
as I discovered intimacy with God and then
as I discovered the joy of His rest.
She knows the depth of the journey
and all the valleys along the way.
I would not have chosen to walk it
on this earth with anyone else.
She truly is my gift from God.

ACKNOWLEDGMENTS

—⁂—

I owe a large debt of gratitude to James Anderson, whose book *For God's Sake, Rest* helped shape my understanding of the pleasure that God's rest can bring to both God and me. I would wholeheartedly recommend reading his book.

I also would like to thank the group of men who went on the first retreat in the Smoky Mountains. We had no idea what God was going to do.

The front cover shows an amazing image of reflection. Sabbath causes us to pause in the presence of the Almighty and learn how to reflect Him in our lives. As my friend James Anderson says, *"If my life is going to clearly reflect the image of God, I am going to have to learn how to rest."*[1]

CONTENTS

—❦❦❦—

Introduction xv
Sabbath Retreat Eve—A Time to Anticipate 1
Day One—A Time to Recalibrate 7
Day Two—A Time of Self-Examination 26
Day Three—A Time of Discovery 47
Day Four—A Time of Joyful Submission 61
Postlude—A Time to Re-enter 76
Weekly Sabbath Plan 83
Principles of the Sabbath 85
Three-Day Retreat Plan 105
Bibliography 107
End Notes 111

INTRODUCTION

D o you need to have intimate time with God?
I want to lovingly and boldly tell you that you must
have intimate time with God if you care to live the life that
you have truly been designed to live. Too many people think
that they can casually listen to others tell them about God
and what should happen in a relationship with Him. That
will not work. I know. I tried that for many years. That way
of relating to God will prevent you from having real truth
take root in your heart. It is your choice.

If you do not get together with God intimately, you will
continue to view Him as either a cosmic genie or as a tyrant
who has unrealistic expectations. You will be bored with God.
You will stay convinced that the universe revolves around
you and your desires. You will stay wrapped up in a very
small story, and your story will be good or bad depending
on how you feel in the moment or what circumstances are
currently in your life. You will miss out on knowing God,
and you will not know peace because your prayers will be
focused around your selfish needs and wants.

But if you take time to consider Jesus and spend time
allowing His truth to permeate and occupy your heart, you
will discover who you truly have been designed to be. The
things in your life that keep you from Him will become
clear. You will confess them, and He will forgive you. You
will understand that He is in control over everything that
is, and you will not be anxious about all the things that may
or could happen. You will not fret over the things that have
happened. His peace will transcend all understanding and

will have new meaning in each moment of the day! The Lord will be near, and your prayers will become filled with gratitude, rejoicing, and thanksgiving because you will know to whom the prayers are offered. You will not just know about God—you will know Him. You will be in an intimate relationship with Him.

If you are reading this, you are about to embark on a retreat to discover what Sabbath rest can bring to your life. You may be moving out of your regular routine for a while, or you may be trying to nestle it into the regular flow of your life. This guidebook is written for a four-day experience, although it can be adapted to best work for your situation.

More than likely, you are among the many who have a misunderstanding of what the Sabbath is and how it can impact your life. You may even have some fear of moving into this journey. Get ready. The Sabbath is one of the greatest gifts that God has created for you.

You will find Him delighting in your decision to accept the gift. It is my prayer that through this retreat journey, you will be struck by the love of the Lord in a new way and that you will long to have the Sabbath become a regular part of your life. If you can set aside at least four days each year for this deeper type of reflection and contemplation, you will find your life with Christ changing and growing in ways you never thought possible, and you will long for regular Sabbath as well.

If you are like me, you will find yourself wanting to have this type of experience one day each week. That is the way God designed it! You will have a longing in your heart to stop each week and spend time with God apart from all the demands of life.

The purpose of this book is twofold. The first is to be a guide for an extended, special encounter with the Lover of your soul. The second is to aid you in considering how you may incorporate the Sabbath into your weekly routine after you spend time discovering what the Sabbath is.

Plan to make this experience very special—a sanctuary in time. I would strongly recommend that you unplug. Leave technology behind as much as possible. Do not call work. Especially leave the computer and the TV behind so that you do not allow your mind to be

PLAN TO MAKE THIS EXPERIENCE VERY SPECIAL—A SANCTUARY IN TIME.

filled with little thoughts. Avoid newspapers and magazines, going shopping, going out to eat, or even going to crowded places. Do not plan a lot of activity. Keep meals simple.

Rest—you may find yourself sleeping more in these days of retreat; that is perfectly fine. You want to come back home rested and refreshed from being with God.

There are many exciting ways to engage in this experience. Some people enjoy the outdoors; others are more comfortable staying inside. Some will engage as couples or in a group; others will go it alone. There is no right or wrong way to enter this experience, but whatever your plans are, make sure you set aside large quantities of time for solitude, silence, and prayer. You are looking to hear from God, and many times He speaks encouragement in a gentle whisper (1 Kings 19:12). I have left many areas open throughout the booklet for journaling.

Each day the reading and Scripture are designed to help your mind focus on a particular thought. Take time to look through and familiarize yourself with the guidebook prior to leaving for the retreat.

It is my prayer that you will come away from this experience changed and empowered because you have been with God differently than ever before.

A poem by A. B. Simpson has impacted me greatly as I have been on this journey of recovering Sabbath rest for my life. It is a poem written at the turn of the twentieth century that describes the beauty that comes from giving away the search for significance in anything other than the intimacy you have been designed to have with Christ. It is the discovery that Jesus is enough. I pray that this Sabbath retreat will bring this awareness to you in a new way, wherever you are in your journey with the Savior.

"Himself" (A. B. Simpson)

Once it was the blessing, Now it is the Lord;
Once it was the feeling, Now it is His Word.
Once His gifts I wanted, Now the Giver own;
Once I sought for healing, Now Himself alone.
Once 'twas painful trying, Now 'tis perfect trust;
Once a half salvation, Now the uttermost.
Once 'twas ceaseless holding, Now He holds me fast;
Once 'twas constant drifting, Now my anchor's cast.
Once 'twas busy planning, Now 'tis trustful prayer;
Once 'twas anxious caring, Now He has the care.
Once 'twas what I wanted, Now what Jesus says;
Once 'twas constant asking, Now 'tis ceaseless praise.
Once it was my working, His it hence shall be;
Once I tried to use Him, Now He uses me.
Once the power I wanted, Now the Mighty One;
Once for self I labored, Now for Him alone.
Once I hoped in Jesus, Now I know He's mine;
Once my lamps were dying, Now they brightly shine.
Once for death I waited, Now His coming hail;
And my hopes are anchored, Safe within the vail.[2]

Sabbath Retreat Eve

A TIME TO ANTICIPATE

———⚬⚬⚬———

A nticipation is a key part of the Sabbath experience. It has been that way for the Israelite people for almost 3,500 years since God gave them the Sabbath as a sign bonding them to Himself (Exodus 31:17). Preparations are made in advance so that twenty minutes before sunset on Friday evening, ready or not, Sabbath begins.

Consider the following passage from Isaiah 58:13–14a and the thoughts that follow.

> *If you keep your feet from breaking the Sabbath and from doing as you please on my holy day, if you call the Sabbath a delight and the LORD's holy day honorable, and if you honor it by not going your own way and not doing as you please or speaking idle words, then you will find your joy in the LORD.*

Clearly God has something to say about the Sabbath. The Sabbath was and is a very special gift from God to man. It is a special day that is to be set aside to be with Him. Think about your childhood. What value was placed on the Sabbath? What are your memories of Sabbath? Write those here.

_____

_____

I remember the Sabbath as a child. We did not refer to it as the Sabbath, but I have come to appreciate that is what it was. Saturday night was bath night. When the morning came, we got dressed in our best clothes and headed off to church.

Although there were very few stores open on Sundays, sometimes we would stop and buy a newspaper at the gas station or go out for lunch at one of the few open restaurants. Afternoons were slow, easy, and relaxing. It was not unusual to spend time with other families and friends. There was often church at night as well.

I remember that we played together as a family, though not the way people play now. Now we call play *leisure*. There was not nearly the same amount of effort or expense required to relax in those days. It was simple play that often just came with being together. The time that we spent together helped us have time to focus on God. Somewhere along the way, life changed, and busyness stepped in to everyday life. Even play began to take a great deal of effort, and rest became less and less valued. I was well along in life before I noticed that I had left something behind—special time each week considering God.

What have your Sabbath experiences been like as an adult? If you have children, what would they say the Sabbath is?

_____

_____

Read Isaiah 58:13–14 again. What does God say the Sabbath is to be about?

Do you find your joy in the LORD? This passage is the only place in Scripture where this exact promise is found. If you keep the Sabbath as God has intended, you will find your joy in the Lord. Has your joy in the Lord been missing? Have you wondered why? God has promised that you can find your joy in Him, but it may require not going your own way on the Sabbath. Could that be true? Do you have any long-lasting experiences of joy related to the Sabbath?

_____

_____

Psalm 37:4 says, *"Delight yourself in the LORD and he will give you the desires of your heart."*

Many times, we get tempted to chase the desires of our heart to bring joy to our lives. That is backwards. In Matthew 6:33, we see what we are designed to be seeking first. We need to learn how to seek God first, spend time with Him first, find comfort from Him first, and find help in any trouble from Him first.

When creation was finished—after the sixth day—God rested (Genesis 2:2). We know that God did not need to rest (Isaiah 40:28). God rested because this was a day that He had blessed and made holy (Genesis 2:3). It was and is to be a day set apart for God.

In his book *The Sabbath*, Abraham Heschel states his view of the significance of the Sabbath's being holy:

> There is no reference in the record of creation to any object in space that would be endowed with the quality of holiness. This is a radical departure from accustomed religious thinking. The mythical mind would expect that, after heaven and earth have been established, God would create a holy place—a holy mountain or a holy spring—whereupon a sanctuary is to be established. Yet it seems as if to the Bible it is *holiness in time*, the Sabbath, which comes first.[3]

3

It is this quote that has led to the title of this guidebook. The sanctuary where you can go to be with God is a place in time! God has given us the Sabbath. He blessed it, and He has made it holy—a *sanctuary in time.* It is a time for you to find your joy in Him and a time for Him to delight in you.

Be very sure, God loves to spend time with you! As Anderson says, "Divine pleasure, not human need is the greatest reason for observing the Sabbath."[4]

Could that be true? Could the Sabbath be focused on how you bless God instead of how He blesses you? This perspective reflects a change in the motive. So many times we try to please God by our activities when it seems that what pleases Him most is our pleasure in being in His presence.

He has told us to observe the Sabbath, and He delights in our obedience (1 Samuel 15:22). I have heard many people say they are not able to get into the rhythm of having a regular, quiet time with God. To them, it seems hard to spend time each day with Him.

I suggest that the reason consistent time spent with God is difficult to establish is because we have not spent time knowing Him in Sabbath. We spend a lot of time getting to know about Him, but do we know Him? So many things cause us to create God in our image. The way that we see Him is distorted. Sabbath is setting aside time to know Him as He truly is, when we can know Him as we experience Him in uninterrupted relationship.

I remember when I met my wife Karen. She found a way into my heart. I could not wait to spend time with her. When we spent time together, it was for getting to know each other deeply. At the time of this writing, we have been married forty-one years. We talk every day. I like to talk to her! I look forward to talking to her, and I look forward to her talking to me, because I have spent special time knowing her. It is the same with my Lord.

Is there someone you look forward to being with every day? Is there something that you look forward to doing every day? Are those the things you are trusting to bring you joy? It is not wrong to find joy in things on this earth. God created the world for our enjoyment and so we could know Him. However, if temporary satisfaction is where you seek to find your primary joy, then things are out of order in your life, and that is not good.

You need the Sabbath. You need quiet time with God so that you can build your love for Him and the relationship that comes from knowing Him intimately. Then, you will be truly known by Him as well (1 Corinthians 8:3).

"Without solitude it is virtually impossible to live a spiritual life. . . . We do not take the spiritual life seriously if we do not set aside some time to be with God and listen to him"[5] (Henri Nouwen).

Try a little exercise. Find a very quiet spot, set a timer, and stop thinking about anything for what you think is 60 seconds.

How long were you silent before you looked again at the clock?

Were you able to stop the clutter of your mind?

This guidebook is designed to lead you through a retreat in which you purposefully set aside blocks of time each day for learning how to stop the clutter of your mind. In the process, hopefully you will learn a way to integrate it into the rhythm of your life. You will have the opportunity to find yourself engaging with His creation and His workmanship differently, if you dare to let go of whatever it is that has kept you from experiencing His presence. How will your life change if you spend quality special time like this with God? It's time to find out!

Day 1
A Time to Recalibrate

———∽∾∽———

F irst and foremost, the Sabbath is a time to dance. It is a time to remember who we are, whose we are, and the joy that remembering those truths will surely bring to our lives! The first day of the retreat is designed to draw us back into the arms of the Lover of our soul and find the delight He has in who we are.

Focus: Joy and Delight—His and ours

"Thou hast made us for thyself, O Lord, and our heart is restless until it finds its rest in thee"[6] (Augustine of Hippo).

"We are far too easily pleased"[7] (C. S. Lewis).

"Above all else, guard your heart, for it is the wellspring of life" (Proverbs 4:23).

What is it that has your heart? We live in a time where busyness overtakes us. We have the technology to stay constantly connected with everyone. It becomes so easy to allow the busyness and the distractions to become the very things that have our heart. We were designed for so much more. What is your heart? We use the heart to define the deepest part of who we are. We give someone our heart and take a risk that they might break it. We long for something deeply, and when it does not come, it causes heartache within us. When we need to talk deeply with someone, we say we need to talk heart-to-heart. When the zeal is gone for some project—or even for life itself—we say that our heart is not in it. Scripture warns us not to lose heart. Your heart is much more than the emotional center of your life. It is more than the organ that beats to keep your blood flowing. The writer of Proverbs tells us that it is the wellspring of life, and as such, we need to guard it. The journey of your heart is the story of your life.

Is it possible that the heart is where we truly experience joy?

When I was a little boy, I asked Jesus to come into my heart. That is how we explained the gospel then. Even as a boy, I knew that I needed something to change in my heart. A few years later, I would learn that my heart is deceitful and desperately wicked to the point of being unknowable (Jeremiah 17:9). I remember those two truths colliding in me, and in many ways, it depicts the conflict in each of our lives. Our desperately wicked, insatiably deceitful heart longs to fulfill itself in ways that do not include God. When that happens, we lose touch with our true heart—the very place God resides within us. We lose the real source of joy, and we find ourselves wrapped up in very small stories. "We are far too easily pleased," as C.S. Lewis stated.

If we were truly able to understand the joy and fulfillment that God longs to bring to our hearts, we would gladly stop the mundane pursuits. And the mundane pursuits take time. They can easily take all our time, and in so doing, spill over into the time that was meant to be spent with the Creator. We have been designed for the joy that comes from a relationship with Him. Any deficiency in the relationship causes restlessness and a lack of joy. We must stop regularly and remind ourselves that we are part of a great story. In the great story,

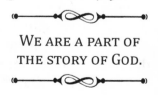

WE ARE A PART OF THE STORY OF GOD.

we once again find the joyous source of our heartbeat. We are a part of the story of God.

God has chosen to write His story and preserve it for countless generations. Have you ever stopped to consider where Moses got his information? We attribute the first lines of the Bible, perhaps the most well-known lines in literature, to him, but he wasn't there. We are told that Moses talked with God face to face (Exodus 33:11). We cannot be sure exactly what that looked like, but I wonder: was it in one of those conversations that God revealed to Moses what those first moments of His story were like? Was there a smile on the face into which Moses looked as the story was recounted? God created with great joy. His joy has not abated. The story starts with love. The story starts in relationship.

"In the beginning God."

God has always been and has always existed in perfect relationship within Himself. From that relationship flowed the creation of man. We have been designed first and foremost for a relationship with God that will move us into joy-filled living. The relationship we have been designed for is a deeply intimate relationship with the triune God. The Trinity is the core of the created order, and that perfect relationship is at the heart of all reality. We long for intimacy because we were created in the image of perfect intimacy.

But that intimacy comes at a price in a fallen world. It involves great risk. It does not take us very long to discover that walls must be built to protect the heart, and soon enough the thought of living from the heart becomes a distant memory, even a forgotten hope. Busyness replaces reflection. Time spent doing replaces time spent relationship building. By default, serving self takes the place of everything else.

There is a distant dream, a past longing that may remind us that we have been made for so much more. But hearing that voice and recognizing that longing requires a kind of solitude and silence that is not easily available or embraced;

there is risk involved, and other voices drown out that call from the heart. We are each designed with a deep-seated desire to be loved for who we are. The Designer has placed the desire there so that we will move to Him—the only One able to love us that way.

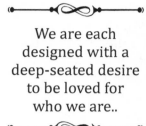

> We are each designed with a deep-seated desire to be loved for who we are..

Self-sufficiency is the thing that keeps us from hearing the voice or believing that the call is real. Self-sufficiency positions the temporary in a place of supremacy above the eternal and causes us to settle for temporary pleasures. Self-sufficiency is what caused Adam and Eve to choose the fruit of the tree above the walk in the garden in the cool of the day. It has not changed since. We rely on our own power, striving, and thoughts to gather and achieve what we want. We do not fully understand that self-sufficiency is pride. Cyril J. Barber has stated, "The self-sufficient do not take time to pray; they merely talk to themselves."[8] It is a lonely existence. It is lonely because it sets aside our heart's desire.

Self-sufficiency also causes us to believe that the joy in God's heart at seeing who we are is somehow dependent upon making ourselves look good for Him. So, we set out on a list of "ought tos" that we believe will please God and, in the process, we miss the relationship. We miss the heart of His joy and the heart of joy He longs for us to have.

Consider Ephesians 1:3–6—Paul's understanding of pre-creation as recounted in The Message:

> *How blessed is God! And what a blessing he is! He's the Father of our Master, Jesus Christ, and takes us to the high places of blessing in him. Long before he laid down earth's foundations, he had us in mind, had settled on us as the focus of his love, to be made whole and*

holy by his love. Long, long ago he decided to
adopt us into his family through Jesus Christ.
(What pleasure he took in planning this!) He
wanted us to enter the celebration of his lavish
gift-giving by the hand of his beloved Son.

Do you see what was going on in the mind of the Trinity prior to the moment He spoke the universe into existence? You! If you are a follower of Jesus, you are His chosen one. You were a focus of His love. You still are. He chose you. He wanted you to enter the celebration of His lavish gift-giving, and He still does. He took pleasure in planning you and your adoption into His family.

Our lives draw us away from basking in this truth. He is jealous for this time. He is jealous for you. All the things that draw your attention from Him are false lovers and joy robbers. Consider some things in your life that have robbed your joy.

Take some time to remember your first love and to dance with the One who knows you best. It is the best first step into Sabbath—recalibrating the heart to remember a truth that was spoken in times past through Asaph the musician who knew the voice of the heart: *"Whom have I in heaven but you? And earth has nothing I desire besides you"* (Psalm 73:25).

Today, recalibrate your journey towards joy and get back on the eternal path! Remind yourself of the relationship you have with Him.

If you keep your feet from breaking the Sabbath
and from doing as you please on my holy day, if
you call the Sabbath a delight and the LORD's
holy day honorable, and if you honor it by not
going your own way and not doing as you
please or speaking idle words, then you will
find your joy in the LORD (Isaiah 58:13–14a).

As you enter this first step of Sabbath, consider these verses from Isaiah. What is your plan for the day ahead of you? What is God's? Are those two plans the same?

Take a moment and answer the questions these verses raise:

How are you planning to call this day a delight?

_____

_____

How are you planning to honor this day?

_____

_____

What are some selfish pleasures that you need to set aside today?

_____

_____

How can you keep from speaking idle words?

_____

_____

These questions are not about where you will be going or what you will be doing. The Sabbath does not require sitting in a musty room with dim lights pouring over some archaic translation of the Bible while fasting and drinking only water, although that is the impression many people have.

The real issue here is what joy God desires for you and Him to experience today. So, the purpose of these questions is not to rob joy from the day; rather, it is to make sure that you do not exchange the permanent joy of the LORD for a lesser temporary joy. Be certain that God is longing for you to find His joy today and every day! He is waiting to lavish it upon you.

If you are involved in a retreat where there are other people around, it is easy to get into idle talk. We long for someone to hear our problems, or we long to solve someone else's problem so that we do not have to focus on our own. There indeed is a place for that, but could I encourage you to remember that you need to learn to talk with and listen to God about these things? We are so used to filling our days with words that we have trouble spending any time in silence.

There are beautiful truths to be found in the joy of solitude and silence with God. Do not confuse solitude with privacy; it is much more. Do not confuse silence with quietness; it is much more. As you learn to practice the disciplines of silence and solitude, you will come to appreciate the depth of the knowledge of God that you will find.

In *Celebration of Discipline*, Richard Foster states, "Loneliness is inner emptiness. Solitude is inner fulfillment."[9] There is a restlessness that longs for solitary time with the Savior in quiet relationship. We can hear the still, small voice of the Lover of our souls as we pull apart from the clutter and distractions of this world. The world we live in is not a world that is sensitive to the love of Christ. Our culture does not radiate His heart. Quite the opposite: it calls to the deepest part of our selfish heart and draws us away from God. It falsely influences our thoughts and perceptions of what is right and wrong. It allows us to judge our spirituality by comparison with others as opposed to the truth of the Word and the heart of the Lord.

Solitude draws us into His arms to be reminded of the truth we have been designed to embrace and live out. We have not been designed for this world in its fallen state. It grates on our very being. Solitude with God brings the peace we so deeply need. This truth is what Paul is relating to his readers in Philippians 4:4–9. Somewhere along the line, we have forgotten the entryway into the peace of God.

It is in solitude and silence that we truly learn how to think about whatever is noble, right, pure, lovely, admirable, or praiseworthy. How many of the conversations that you are a part of or that you overhear have those qualities at the core? God's side of every one of your conversations with Him does. He speaks beautiful truth into your life. The key is to find a solitary place for Him to speak that is also quiet enough, so you can hear.

Remember that His Word pierced the silence. First the Word pierced the silence in the dawn of creation; then, in the fullness of time following 400 years of deafening silence, that same Word became flesh and dwelt among us (John 1:1–14). In so doing, He became a visible expression of the thoughts of God. Allow some silence to come into your day so that the Word of God may pierce it.

COME TO THE POINT WHERE INSTEAD OF READING SCRIPTURE, YOU ARE ALLOWING SCRIPTURE TO READ YOU.

Come to the point where instead of reading Scripture, you are allowing Scripture to read you.

Consider Proverbs 4:23: *"Above all else, guard your heart, for it is the wellspring of life."*

What does it mean to guard your heart? How have you left your heart unguarded? How has that allowed lesser gods to have a part of your heart?

_____

_____

Ask God to reveal to you what has grabbed your heart other than Him. This can be one or many things. These can be things that go back very far in your life. Ask God to reveal to you those things that have shaped your heart. Ask God to reveal how the things other than Himself have kept you from giving your heart to Him. Talk with God about how these things affect your view of Him.

The things that have shaped our hearts apart from God are the things that cause us to live in a very small story. They cause us to think very small thoughts and strive for very small hopes and dreams. They cause us to settle for temporary happiness instead of the eternal joy found in Him. God desires for you to delight in His presence as He delights in yours. He desires for you to pursue that pleasure relentlessly. At some level you know this is true. It is part of the reason that you are on this retreat!

Sometimes I get overwhelmed when I think that God chose me before the foundation of the world was put in place (remember Ephesians 1:2–6 earlier in this chapter). I would not have chosen me. I look back, and I can see where I was trying to make myself unchoosable in many ways! Yet, God lavishes me with love. If I am to fully know that lavished love, I need to take my heart back from the false lovers and allow myself to experience the fullness of the love of God. Doing so allows me to dance in His presence.

What thoughts come to your heart as you consider the passage from Ephesians 1?

Consider joy for a few moments. What things bring you joy?

Why do these things bring you joy?

_____

_____

_____

_____

What does it mean to find your joy in the LORD?

_____

_____

_____

_____

What keeps you from finding joy and delight in Him?
(These are the lesser lovers that have your heart.)

_____

_____

_____

_____

What has robbed your joy?

_____

_____

_____

_____

Following are some verses and passages that speak about joy and delight. Consider the truths in these verses throughout the day. Let His Word speak into your life. Spend your day looking specifically for ways to delight yourself in the presence of the LORD and to consider the way He delights in you. This can be very hard the first time you try it, especially if you have grown used to filling your life with things that keep you from delighting in Him. Past hurts, failures, regrets, incorrect teaching, and misunderstandings may have dulled your heart to the joy available in His presence. You can allow yourself to be defined by the things that have defeated you, which will keep you from hearing the song that God is singing over you. Delighting in the Lord is worth the effort and will become one of the things you most anticipate in Sabbath time. Learn to hear and listen to the song your Lord is singing over you!

LEARN TO HEAR AND LISTEN TO THE SONG YOUR LORD IS SINGING OVER YOU!

The LORD your God is with you, he is mighty to save. He will take great delight in you, he will quiet you with his love, he will rejoice over you with singing. Zephaniah 3:17

Read the following passages and journal any thoughts that you may have in response. What do you learn about joy and delight?

Psalms 16:2,11; 28:7; 33:1–3; 31:7; 47:1–9; 66:1–5; 71:22–23; 92:1–4; 94:18–19; 98:1–9; 126:1–6

_____

_____

_____

_____

_____

John 15 (focus on verse 11)

_____

_____

_____

_____

Do you know the joy of the Lord in you?

_____

_____

Nehemiah 8:5–12 (focus on verse 11)
How is the joy of the Lord your strength?

_____

_____

_____

_____

_____

Psalm 149:4–5 (continue reading through 150:6)

_____

_____

_____

_____

_____

Isaiah 61:10–11; 62:5
What feelings rise up in the depths of your heart as you read these verses?

_____

_____

_____

_____

Isaiah 65:17–19

Jeremiah 9:23–24

Romans 15:13

Galatians 5:22-23

_____

_____

_____

_____

_____

Finally, think about your heart. We started today thinking about various metaphors that involve the heart. Can you think of some that were not listed earlier?

_____

_____

Scripture lists several for us. One of those is an undivided heart. Consider two passages that speak of an undivided heart: Psalm 86:11–13 and Ezekiel 11:19. Are there any ways in which your heart is divided?

_____

_____

_____

_____

_____

Do you remember a time when you asked Jesus to come into your heart? What did that mean to you? What does it mean now?

_____

_____

_____

_____

_____

The church at Ephesus experienced what we call *heart drift*. They left their first love. Read Revelation 2:1–5 and compare it to Ephesians 3:14–19. Is there any way in which your heart has drifted?

_____

_____

_____

_____

_____

Earlier, I wrote about the time that I asked Jesus to come into my heart. It was a very special moment for me. I asked Him to forgive all the sins that I had committed, and I asked Him to be my Savior. I placed my trust in Him. Looking back now, I can see that rather than giving Him my heart, I had Him move in among all that was already there. My heart was divided in many ways. Perhaps it is the same for you. Perhaps today, you have seen that in many ways you have been seeking joy, delight, and satisfaction in many other places. That is the defining characteristic of a divided heart.

If you have truly asked Jesus to come into your heart, the deepest meaning comes when you have given Him your whole heart and resolved to follow Him alone. You become a follower of Jesus.

Journal closing thoughts and a prayer as you come to the end of Day 1.

Day 1 Journal Questions:

What did you experience today as you exposed your heart before God?

_____

_____

Can you recount a special way in which He met you?

_____

_____

What did you learn about yourself?

_____

_____

In what ways are you more filled with genuine joy?

_____

_____

Write a brief prayer expressing your heart.

_____

_____

Day 2
TIME OF SELF-EXAMINATION

———∽∽∽———

A fter a time of recalibrating, it is time to identify the things
that keep us from experiencing our in the LORD and to
turn away from them. It is what is known as repentance.

Focus: Repentance and Brokenness

"When our Lord and Master, Jesus Christ, said, "Repent,"
He called for the entire life of believers to be one of repentance" (#1 of the 95 Theses, Martin Luther).

"It is true to say that the greatest of sins is to be conscious of no sin; but a sense of need will open the door to
the forgiveness of God"[10] (William Barclay).

"God's kindness leads you towards repentance"
(Romans 2:4).

"To be broken is the beginning of revival. It is painful, it
is humiliating, but it is the only way"[11] (Roy Hession).

*"Let us throw off everything that hinders and the sin that
so easily entangles"* (Hebrews 12:1).

"Repentance is a prerequisite to rest. Rest requires repentance as an admittance fee. We may attempt to enter the rest
of God while our innards churn with sin, but Sabbath-rest

will remain a locked door. Sabbath-rest is a pleasure of God we cannot enter apart from repentance of sin and a change of heart"[12] (James Anderson).

"And because you Gentiles have become his children, God has sent the Spirit of his Son into your hearts, and now you can call God your dear Father" (Galatians 4:6, NLT).

"Jesus replied, 'If anyone loves me, he will obey my teaching. My Father will love him, and we will come to him and make our home with him'" (John 14:23).

"So that Christ may dwell in your hearts through faith" (Ephesians 3:17).

The quotes and verses above help us understand what it means to have Jesus come into our hearts—to become a follower of Jesus. To become a follower of Jesus, a person must come to a point in their lives when they repent and choose to accept Jesus as their own personal Savior and King. At that moment they move into an exchanged life. Their hearts are changed from stone to flesh. Their hearts become the home of the triune God. I pray that you have done that!

As we think of Christ dwelling in our hearts, it causes us to think what kind of home it is for Him. I sometimes wonder what He does among the clutter of our hearts. The core of who we are is so easily manipulated by what we think others want from us. Our heart has experienced many wounds, more from our own thoughts than those of others. In the song "In The Light," Charlie Peacock calls this phenomenon "the disease of self run[ning] through my blood, a cancer fatal to my soul."[13] It is the disease of self that must be repented. Those thoughts and desires are the old

WE HAVE SPENT A GREAT DEAL OF TIME FURNISHING OUR HEARTS INAPPROPRIATELY.

furnishings of our hearts. The new Tenant has brought much better furnishings. As a matter of fact, He is ready to completely remodel. He is waiting for our permission. Repentance is that permission, and brokenness is the opening of the hands to release what we have been gripping. That release comes with the acknowledgement that what we have been holding on to is damaging to us.

But it is very hard. It is hard for many reasons. We have spent a great deal of time furnishing our hearts inappropriately. We know that our hearts need a makeover, but we are afraid of the unknown. So, we hold on to the things that have hurt us in the past, hoping that somehow if we keep them, they will bring healing. We hold on to the hurtful things that bring a momentary rush of pleasure, followed by unrelenting shame. Jesus is waiting to clear the heart of all those things and fill it with the aroma of His love and unconditional acceptance.

This is what our heart is waiting for. But the old tenants will not be easily evicted, especially if we are trying to evict those desires ourselves. We are unable. As ironic as it is, those harmful thoughts and desires have become precious to us, and we cannot in our own strength remove them. We have become very fond of them. Jesus knows that. He is waiting for the word from us to go to work and remove all those things. That is what we can do. We can give Him permission. Our permission brings His action. That is what free will requires. It requires that we choose Him above all other lovers of our own volition. We turn from wanting those things to wanting Christ instead. That is repentance.

King David was a man who understood how unconfessed sin can block us from the Father. He learned that lesson in his sin with Bathsheba and subsequent confrontation with God through Nathan (2 Samuel 11–12). His confession and repentance are recorded in Psalm 51: *"Create in me a clean heart, O God."* I do not think there is any way for us to understand fully how God longs to fulfill that request.

Alan Kraft points out how good we are at not seeing the depth of our sin. He uses the analogy of an iceberg. Seven-eighths of the iceberg lies under water. It is not possible for us to see the bulk of it from the surface. Kraft says that we spend a great deal of time focused on the small part of sin that we see, ignoring the massive amount that is in the core of who we are.[14]

We must come to a point where we understand that we are totally depraved. Our hearts are wicked and deceitful. There is nothing in our old selves that is good enough for God. That could seem discouraging, if it weren't for the fact that it just proves we need a Savior! We must realize the depth of our sinful nature and the control it has over us, or we will not repent. We will continue to pridefully look at the polished surface (Matthew 23:27) and convince ourselves that everything is all right. Apparently, that is how David spent the year prior to Nathan's coming to see him. I am sure that he knew that all was not right. We all do.

When we are talking badly about someone so we can look better, when we are exaggerating a story, when we are gossiping about someone, when we are overly concerned about defending ourselves, complaining, shifting the blame onto someone else, or seeking our own gain above anyone else, we know that it is not right. But our pride causes us to refuse to see it.

To enter the presence of God intimately requires that we rid ourselves of the filth of our sin through broken repentance. It can even mean that we need to repent of some of the "good things" that we have done. Good things done for the wrong reasons are sin. Our motive is God's concern. Man looks at the outward appearance—God looks at the heart (1 Samuel 16:7). Many of the right things we do are done so that we will look good or so that we will be noticed or so that someone will do something for us. These are all sinful motives that make the actions themselves sinful.

Today we enter a time of repentance. We will be asking God to reveal to us those deep parts of our lives that are sin—the core things in our hearts. We are remodeling today!

Please begin by reading Psalm 139.

In this psalm, David does a masterful job of revealing to us how to seek for and experience repentance. He begins by acknowledging that God does indeed search us all the time. He is constantly watching us, and He knows us intimately. David sees that as a cause for great celebration and makes it obvious throughout this psalm.

God knows you far better than you know yourself. He is already intimately aware of everything you will bring to Him today. He knows you completely. Celebrate that fact. Celebrate the fact that He is familiar with all your ways: the way you handle criticism, the way you drive, the way you think about others—all your ways. Celebrate the fact that He knows what you are going to say before you say it! Celebrate that He took the time to knit you together and that He is glad He did.

Sometimes people get confused because of verses 19–22 in this chapter. Could I suggest that you think of that section as your crying out to God against the very things that you want to repent of, the things that you hate in your life because they are opposed to God's touch and are the adversaries that speak against God with evil intent? Ask God to slay them!

You need to ask Him what He sees as He examines you because God made you, loves you, knows you, and wants the best for you! This becomes clear in verses 23 and 24. It is in those verses that David—a man blameless before the Lord—asked God to reveal what He had found in the examination. Many times, people do not care to know. God is ready to reveal the areas of your life that are keeping you from Him, but you need to ask Him to do so. Then you must be ready to listen and change.

This is repentance at its core. Ask God to search you and reveal the areas that need to change; then agree with Him, ask Him to forgive, and ask for the power and ability to take the necessary steps to change. Further, you need to renounce the control of that area over your life. Do this verbally—out loud so that Satan can hear you—claim the victory in the name of Jesus.

This will be a time of deep reflection. It is best done in solitude and silence in the careful, loving hands of Jesus. This is probably the most intense day, but it is absolutely necessary. It is very important throughout the day, as David demonstrated, that you consider how special you are to God. When you stand exposed before God, you need to remember who you are in Him so that you will not fall into the trap of the accuser. Remember Jesus sits at the right hand of the Father, deflecting any accusations that may come (Romans 8:34). Remember that Jesus is bigger than any mistake!

> *"My dear children, I write this to you so that you will not sin. But if anyone does sin, we have one who speaks to the Father in our defense—Jesus Christ, the Righteous One. He is the atoning sacrifice for our sins"* (1 John 2:1–2a).

It is a time to take a real look inside of who you are. This is critical if you are to be in the presence of the Lord in Sabbath. This is consecration. It is important to ask yourself some tough questions on the pages that follow. Be honest. Pray and ask God to reveal to you the depths of your heart and who you really are. Then you will be ready to engage with Him.

This will be a long day. Take your time. Take breaks for prayer walks. If you feel that you cannot get through all the questions, take the ones that seem most relevant to you at this moment. You may end up on one revealed sin for a long season. Old habits die very hard. God is patient with you. Remember that it is His kindness that leads you to repentance (Romans 2:4).

The following questions are designed to get to the layers of the iceberg that are below the surface. They are penetrating questions that are not very often asked. Their purpose is to help you look at things in a different light. You must not wink at sin. You cannot rationalize it away as a struggle or character flaw or personality trait. You must call it what it is and turn away from it. Consider what level of sin you have allowed yourself to become comfortable with in your life.

Answer each question with total honesty and then agree with God as He reveals truth. Confess; be willing to make it right and forsake it. Praise God for the healing and cleansing touch, and then accept His forgiveness. Celebrate His touch and the new intimacy that this cleansing brings.

Genuine Relationship with Christ (2 Corinthians 13:5)
Are you genuinely saved? Have you truly placed your trust in Christ alone for your eternal security? Have you completely surrendered to Him as your LORD and Savior? Are there any ways in which you have just added Jesus to everything else in your life? Is Jesus Christ in you? Are you truly a follower of Jesus?

_____

_____

_____

_____

_____

The Word of God (Joshua 1:8; Psalm 119:11, 97)
Do you love the Word of God? Do you meditate on it? Does it draw you? Do you find it to be alive and meaningful for your life? Do you have a meaningful devotion time that is consistent? Do you just read the Bible, or do you let the Bible read you?

_____

_____

_____

_____

Forgiveness (Ephesians 4:32; Colossians 3:13)
Is there any unforgiveness in your heart? Is there anyone you are harboring a grudge against? Is there anything for which you have not forgiven someone? Do you have a heart that seeks to forgive? Are you living in the forgiveness you have received in Jesus?

_____

_____

_____

_____

Bitterness (Ephesians 4:31)
Has any type of bitterness grown inside you? Are you able to rejoice with those who rejoice, even if they get something that you think you deserve?

_____

_____

_____

_____

_____

The Tongue (Psalm 19:14; Luke 6:43–45;
Ephesians 4:29)
Is there any unwholesome talk that comes from your mouth?
Do you use sarcasm easily? Are you cynical in your communication? How does that impact your communication with
others? Are the words of your mouth pleasing to the Lord?
Do you intentionally think of how you can use your words
to build others up? How are the words that you regularly
speak beneficial for those who are listening?

_____

_____

_____

_____

_____

Truthfulness (Ephesians 4:25)
Do you speak truthfully to others? Do you ever exaggerate
when telling a story? Do you ever "spin" a story when telling
it so that others take your side? Do you ever use silence to
avoid speaking truth?

_____

_____

_____

_____

_____

Anger (Ephesians 4:26, 31)
Do you have issues with uncontrolled anger and fits of rage? Is there any anger that lies under the surface in any area of your life?

_____

_____

_____

_____

_____

Moral Purity (Ephesians 5:3–4)
Do you find yourself thinking about immoral things? Do you keep yourself from any media that may cause you to fanta-size about morally impure things? Is your conversation clean and pure? Is your behavior above reproach? Do you use foul language? Are there any things that God finds detestable that you consider entertainment? Do you view pornography?

_____

_____

_____

_____

_____

_____

_____

_____

Witness (Matthew 28:18–20; Mark 5:19–20)
Are you telling others about Christ verbally? Do you have a ready testimony to tell others of what Jesus has done and is doing in your life? Do you mourn for those who do not know Jesus? Are you more concerned about how someone has treated you than you are about his or her relationship with Christ?

_____

_____

_____

_____

_____

_____

_____

Selflessness (Philippians 2:3–4)
Do you think primarily of yourself? Do you consider the needs of others? Is your attitude the same as Christ's? Is there any way in which selfish ambition drives you?

_____

_____

_____

_____

_____

Compassion (Matthew 9:36; Ephesians 4:32)
Do you have a heart that looks with compassion on others? Are you quicker to judge a person or to see the person as one who needs a touch from Jesus? Do you ever ache for the needs of another? Have you positioned yourself to be too busy to be kind?

_____

_____

_____

_____

_____

I want to stop for a moment here. Remember that it is the kindness of God that leads us to repentance. Sometimes when we look at questions like these, they can overwhelm us. We can either breeze through them in avoidance, perceiving ourselves as good, or we can get overcome with the depth of our sin, overly focusing on each question in condemnation. Neither of these responses are helpful. God's desire is for you to see the truth and truly repent. He desires for you to confess and accept the forgiveness that He offers with deep appreciation. One who is forgiven much loves much.

Please read the account of the woman at Simon's house (Luke 7:36–50). The way Jesus responds is worth thinking about here. The attitude of Simon reveals that if we see ourselves as being better than we are, we will miss the gift of forgiveness and be unable to love Jesus because we have not fully seen our need for His love. If you have been breezing over the questions and not asking God to reveal what He has seen, this may be your attitude.

However, the attitude of the woman in this story displays a heart that understands the depth of its sinfulness and is swept away in love that transcends the trappings of this world. When we reach this same point, we can connect with Jesus at the level He longs for as we embrace the forgiveness offered through His amazing grace. The person who recognizes the greatness of the debt that has been paid by the sacrifice of Christ will be far more in love with Him. If you have seen your sin in these questions and sought forgiveness from God, you have felt that release and that love.

Each of these questions provides you the choice to fall more deeply in love with Jesus or build a larger wall. Truthful answers reveal whatever it is that keeps you from allowing Jesus to have your full heart. Answering the questions honestly and asking for the cleansing forgiveness freely given will create a clean heart in you. It will crush your heart of stone. You will then have a contrite heart, a broken heart—which God will then revive as He indwells your heart. He is in your heart for that specific reason—revival (Isaiah 57:15)!

Consider a few more questions.

Sacrifice (Luke 9:23–24; Philippians 3:7–8)
Are you ready to sacrifice whatever you must for the cause of Christ and for others? Do you give only from your excess of time, talents, and funds? Have you put your earthly desires aside for God's?

_____

_____

_____

_____

_____

Clear Conscience (Matthew 5:23–24; Acts 24:16)
Is there anyone who has a legitimate claim against you that you have avoided? Have you broken any promises to your family or friends? Is there anyone in your life from whom you need to seek forgiveness? Jot down those names and prepare your heart to seek forgiveness.

_____

_____

_____

_____

_____

Idolatry (1 Corinthians 10:14–22)
Is there anything that you have given your heart to other than God? Is there anything that has most of your thoughts? Is there anything that you can't stop thinking about? Is there anything you want more than God? What are you worshiping?

_____

_____

_____

_____

_____

Motives (1 Samuel 16:7)
Are your motives pure? Do you have a hidden or personal agenda in any of the things that you do? Do you act differently around people than you do when you are alone to impress them?

_____

_____

_____

_____

_____

Clean Heart (1 John 1:9)
Are you willing to let go of all sin for God? Are you able to confess your sin by name, or do you use generalities? Do you keep short accounts with God? Does your sin grieve you? When you confess, do you believe that God has forgiven you, or do you continue to live in defeat, guilt, and shame?

_____

_____

_____

_____

_____

Spirit-filled (Ephesians 5:18)
Is there anything besides the Holy Spirit that is controlling your life? Any addictions? Are you continually seeking the presence of the Holy Spirit in your life?

_____

_____

_____

_____

_____

Prayer (1 Thessalonians 5:17)
Are you in a state of constant communication with God? Are you lifting others up in intercession? Are you seeking for God's will to be done? If God were to answer your prayers, what would change?

_____

_____

_____

_____

_____

Humility (Philippians 2:3)
Do you consider all others above yourself? Do you focus on the failures of others or your own faults? Do you look down on anyone? Do you desire to be served? Do you consider yourself to be approachable when criticism is needed? Do you ever try to cover up a sin? Do you avoid humiliation?

_____

_____

_____

_____

_____

Discipleship (2 Timothy 2:2)
Are you intentionally investing in the life of another by passing on truth to them? Are you learning so that you can teach? Do you have a mentor in your life who is imparting God's wisdom into your life? Do you listen to that person?

_____

_____

_____

_____

_____

Gluttony (Proverbs 23:20–21)
Do you involve yourself in excessive indulgence of any kind? Do you give yourself to any pleasure without restraint?

_____

_____

_____

_____

_____

As you close out your day, read two psalms that speak of the journey you have been on today: Psalms 32 and 51. These are two prayers that David writes after his time of confession. They have been preserved by God to bring you peace.

*"When we were overwhelmed by sins, you forgave our transgressions (*Psalm 65:3).

If your sin has seemed overwhelming, remember that in Jesus, it can all be forgiven!

This is not a new journey, as you know. It began when Adam and Eve acknowledged their sin and God forgave. Their sin caused them to cover up and hide, but the loving touch of God brought restoration and reconciliation. It does not mean that the consequences of the choices are removed, but the sin, guilt, and shame are taken away as far as the east is from the west.

Journal closing thoughts and a prayer as Day 2 ends.

Day 2 Journal Questions:

What did you experience today as you exposed your heart before God?

_____

_____

Can you recount a special way in which He met you?

_____

_____

What did you learn about yourself?

_____

_____

Did you experience freedom as you allowed God to begin the remodeling project?

_____

_____

Write a brief prayer expressing your heart.

_____

_____

Special note: This day may have opened some areas that you have kept concealed for a long time. It may have exposed areas that you were unaware of. It may have revealed that there are people who you need to forgive or people you need to seek forgiveness from, and you do not know how. You may need help doing this. If so, seek your pastor or another trusted godly mentor to walk the journey with you.

Day 3
A TIME OF DISCOVERY

———— ∽∽∽ ————

Having cleansed ourselves in the fountain of forgiveness, it is now time to bask in the beauty of who God is in a fresh way. Now we can see Him with our heart.

Focus: Discovering the joy of knowing God more deeply

"My ears had heard of you but now my eyes have seen you" (Job 42:5).

"Now this is eternal life, that they may know you, the only true God and Jesus Christ, whom you have sent" (John 17:3).

"I keep asking that the God of our Lord Jesus Christ, the glorious Father, may give you the Spirit of wisdom and revelation, so that you may know him better" (Ephesians 1:17).

"What comes to mind when we think about God is the most important thing about us"[15] (A. W. Tozer).

It has been said that God created man in His image and that man has been returning the favor ever since. We have come to a point where it is very hard to fathom who God is apart from the influence of man's thoughts. It is easiest for us to determine that God is like us—only much greater. So, when we consider His attributes and characteristics, it is only natural for us to start from what we know—us. But God is not natural; He is supernatural.

There is a mysticism to God that cannot and should not be overlooked. He is at the same time unknowable in all of who He is, and yet knowable inasmuch as He has revealed Himself to us. It is in many ways unthinkable to consider that God would allow us the privilege of knowing Him. Yet, we must remember that knowing Him is why we have been created. Relationship presumes knowledge on the part of both persons. We know God, and He knows us (Galatians 4:9). The design is for that knowledge to be intimate in nature.

Knowing and being known intimately is not something that comes easily to us because sin needs to hide. We feel a need to conceal those things inside of us that we know are wrong. That is the beauty of the exercise we went through yesterday. God has no sin, and we have no sin of which He is unaware. Confession allows us to come out of hiding and back into the light of glorious relationship.

How is it that we can come to know God? Without the truth of Scripture all we have are our own thoughts about who He is. We are then left to either spend great effort or marginal effort trying to know about Him. This is rather like being married without actually knowing your spouse but only knowing what others have said about him or her

Knowing a great God means that we must think great thoughts and think about a great story. The story of God— His story as revealed in His Word—puts Him and His purposes at the center, requiring a big paradigm shift for us. After birth, it doesn't take long for us to begin to think of ourselves as the center of all there is. God is reduced to the One who will take care of the things in our lives that we need and are unable to handle ourselves.

Moralistic therapeutic deism, a term first coined by an American sociologist Christian Smith, is the false thought that God's only demand of us is that we be nice and that His goal is for us to be happy and to feel good. He is not needed in daily life except to solve the various issues or problems that come up—sort of a cosmic magic genie. He owes heaven to all good people.[16] Sadly, this is very close to the definition most contemporary Western evangelicals have of God.

It is critical for us to know the one true God as He has revealed Himself in Scripture. Knowing God as He is requires examination of Scripture. That is why it is so important to love the Word of God and to long for time to read and study and memorize. This can seem dull to many.

Theology has come to mean the study of God and His relation to the world. The internationally renowned priest and author Henri Nouwen points out that the original meaning for the word was "union with God in prayer."[17] That definition more truly expresses my heart toward theology. I want to have theology maintain a mystical aspect so that the Spirit of God shapes my heart. He is the one who inspired the text, illuminates the meaning, and empowers me for the implementation of its truth into my life. Today we will look at theology. We will examine the attributes of God, but we will do so in union with God in prayer.

Today we will look at some of the attributes of God as revealed in Scripture. We will look at a very brief explanation of each attribute. Then, most importantly, I will ask you to join with God in prayer from the heart to consider how that attribute can impact your life in new and refreshing ways. Ponder each attribute carefully. Have a conversation with God about each attribute. Ask Him to have each attribute draw you closer to Him and to bring you to a place of greater awe.

This is an especially good day to ponder His workmanship. It is a time to set your work aside and gaze at His! Try to get out into nature for today's lesson and contemplate the incredible detail that goes into all His creation. If He pays such attention to detail in the lesser parts of His creation, how intimately involved do you think He is in your life? Spend a great deal of time "stopping to smell the roses."

Listen to the birds and all the sounds of creation—God does. Inhale with a deep breath the aroma of the earth—God does. Focus more on the taste of each thing that you choose to eat today.

Look deeply at the beauty of each thing that He has created. Touch the softness of a flower; find all different types of textures that you can feel.

Think about the diversity of creation and consider the harmony that diversity affords. Remind yourself that He spoke the original design into existence from nothing so that you could know Him. Read Hebrews 11:3 and Psalm 19:1–6.

Spend a moment and write a prayer to Him thanking Him for His creation work. Be specific.

_____

_____

Learning to see God for who He is draws us into union with Him through prayer. It is continual prayer in which we talk to Him about the things we see. By this time in the retreat you are probably getting used to the idea of being away from technology. I hope that you have been able to make that choice. If so, you have probably discovered something long ago forgotten. In his book *Long Wandering Prayer*, Pastor David Hansen recounts the experience of a woman who spoke of the importance of being in nature and away from technology:

> "Observing [nature] helped me realize deep within me how congruent the natural world is with my soul, unlike the world of technology that seems so grating and unnatural—incongruent—with that still, small voice of God within me."[18]

Have you sensed in a new way that technology can grate on you? It is natural for us to have a longing to walk with our Lord in the garden and chat with Him in the cool of the day. It is there that His soft voice can be relished. You may want to start by just walking and looking. It may be that is all you get to do today. Make it a day to focus on Him and His splendor.

Consider how much more at home you feel away from all the technology that whistles in your ears during your regular daily rhythm. Consider how much calmer you feel without the commotion of everyday life and pressures. Really take time to consider how you fit into creation and God's plan. Fold yourself into the palm of His hand.

FOLD YOURSELF INTO THE PALM OF HIS HAND.

Creation has been subjected to frustration because of sin, yet you can perceive the remaining fingerprint of God as you stop, look, and listen. Intentionally put aside thoughts about your work so that you may consider His work in a new and fresh way.

Scriptures I would encourage you to read throughout the day include Psalm 33, Psalm 65, and Isaiah 40.

Make sure to also spend a special amount of time in Job 38:1–42:6. As you read this passage, consider your mighty, awesome, and holy God. When Job asked why, God answered with who. Carefully read this passage as a loving God's explanation of just how much attention He pays to every detail in the world. Allow that to comfort you. Recognize that if He is watching over all creation in this manner, He must be watching over each of the details of your life even more!

Look carefully at the attributes listed on the following pages. Considering these attributes can have an incredible impact on your life and your perception of who God really is.

Consider the glories of God's majesty and write down your thoughts as you speak to God and He reveals a new awareness of His awesome splendor. Praise Him for His greatness. Join in union with Him through prayer. Think about how knowing God more deeply brings the joy of discovery into your heart.

God is (Genesis 1:1; Exodus 3:14).
"In the beginning, God."
Think about that small sentence for a moment or a day. Contemplate the reality of the truth expressed. God is. When He starts to tell His story, He does not explain any more about Himself other than that He is and He always has been. In the beginning, God. He is the Great I AM. He is always existing in the eternal present. God is. What impact does that have on who you are and how you view your life?

God is holy (Psalm 99:9; Isaiah 6:1–3).
The holiness of God is that attribute which sets Him apart from all that is. It is His divine holiness that causes Him to be unique, unapproachable, and incomprehensible. His holiness cannot even be imagined. It was God's holiness that caused Isaiah to see himself for who he really was. All illusions of right standing are laid bare before the holiness of God. How does considering the holiness of God give you a fresh passion for worshipping Him? What is your response to the holiness of God when you consider Isaiah's?

_____

_____

_____

_____

_____

_____

_____

God is ever-present (Psalm 46:1, 139:7–12;
Matthew 28:20b).
While the holiness of God is real and expresses His tran-
scendence, just as real is the fact that He is immanent. He is
always here with you. He is near to you. He will never leave
you. Consider the immanence of God. Do you ever act in such
a way that would indicate you do not think God is with you?
Do you ever think that God is unaware of what is happening
in your life, good or bad? Does His presence bring you peace?

_____

_____

_____

_____

_____

God is all-powerful (Psalm 89:9–13; 1 John 4:4).
The all-powerful attribute of God is known as His omnipotence. He holds absolute power over all things. There is absolutely nothing in all of creation that is more powerful than God or that has power over God. He is supreme in power. His power can bring victory to anything that comes into your life. Are there any habits or addictions over which you feel victory is not possible? Do you put your trust in your strength to accomplish something, or do you trust in the strength of God flowing through you (Psalm 20:7)? Do you believe that God is able to change any person?

God is all-knowing (Psalm 139:1–2; 1 John 3:20).
All-knowing refers to the omniscience of God. God knows everything there is to be known. There is nothing that is outside of His knowledge. This includes all the things that will be, could be, might be, might not be, and could never be. It includes all that ever was and all that ever will be. He has complete knowledge of it all. He has never needed to learn anything, and He never will. Who do you go to for advice on a situation in your life? Do you go to God first or to friends? Do you study the Word of God regularly and faithfully to seek answers to your questions? Do you give advice based on your wisdom, or do you reflect on God's truth first?

_____

_____

_____

_____

God is love (Romans 5:8; 1 John 4:16).
God's love is complete. It has no beginning, and it has no end. It has no limit and no conditions. There is no way that created beings can make themselves more lovable to God, and there is no way that created beings can make themselves unlovable to God. His lovingkindness extends to all He has made (Psalm 145:13). His love is His unconditional affection. He is committed to the well-being of the objects of His affection. Do you ever feel as though you have slipped out of the love of God? Does the love of God in you cause you to love others genuinely? Do you realize that God in His love is committed to your well-being, even as He may bring correction into your life? Do you feel unconditionally loved by God, or do you feel His love is based in some way upon your performance?

_____

_____

_____

_____

_____

_____

_____

_____

God is unchanging (Psalm 102:25–27; Malachi 3:6; James 1:17).

God is immutable. He cannot and will not and does not change. He is perpetually the same. He can be counted on to be always who He was, who He is, and who He has revealed Himself to be. He can therefore be trusted. When you consider all the things in your life that change, how does it cause you to think about the immutability of God? What confidence does it bring into your life? What are you tempted to rely upon?

_____

_____

_____

_____

God is faithful (Deuteronomy 7:9; 2 Thessalonians 3:3).

God will always keep His promises. This is an absolute certainty. The faithfulness of God allows assurance of hope in the future. He has gone before, and He will do what He has said He will do. Do you believe that God has provided a way out of each of your temptations (1 Corinthians 10:13)? Do you fully trust in the reliability of the promise of God even when it requires great patience? What peace comes to you as you consider the faithfulness of God?

_____

_____

_____

_____

_____

God is just (Genesis 18:25; Psalm 97:2; Romans 3:25–26, 9:14).

God does not just follow a standard of justice. He is the standard. As such, all that He is and all that He does is done with integrity and fairness. God's justice demands moral equity in the final analysis. God's justice assures us that one day the scales will be balanced. Do you ever complain about being treated unfairly? Do you believe that God is just in all His ways? Are you able to rejoice with those who rejoice even when you feel they are taking something that should have been yours? Do you realize that you can be content trusting that God is just in all His decisions?

_____

_____

_____

_____

God is good (Exodus 33:19–20; Psalm 34:10, 84:11; Romans 2:4).

The goodness of God is His disposition to be kind in all that He does and in all His thoughts. He is filled with good will, benevolence, tenderheartedness, and a quickness to forgive and show compassion. He takes great pleasure in the happiness of His people. It is His goodness that causes Him to desire to be generous. Do you see how the goodness of God is touching every aspect of your life? Are you quick to see that His goodness is what causes you to see your need to repent? Do you see that His goodness longs to keep you from the things that would bring you harm? How much joy does it bring you to worship a God that is good and has good thoughts about and toward you?

Have you found yourself being swept away in worship as you have considered the attributes of God? Worship flows from a proper understanding of God. But what is worship? As a very basic definition, *worship* is ascribing worth to something or someone. Worship is what we have been designed for. Read Revelation 4 and 5 as you conclude your day. These two chapters give a very small glimpse into what worship is like in the throne room of God (the place where

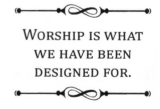

WORSHIP IS WHAT
WE HAVE BEEN
DESIGNED FOR.

your prayers are taken). This passage describes what worship is like when there is no sin to get in the way of recognizing the incredible worth of Holy God Almighty. Be very sure that if you have been truly reborn, your new spirit worships God in the manner described in these two chapters and will do so forever.

What would happen if you were able to literally be in the throne room of God? How would you respond? Would it be any different than the way you respond now when you consider God?

You can begin to live your life intentionally conscious of the presence of God as you begin to consciously consider and appreciate these and all the other attributes of God and meditate on how majestic He is.

The flesh places value and worth on temporary things above God. That is the definition of idolatry. This includes thoughts about God that are not worthy of Him—casual acknowledgment as opposed to adoration—especially as it relates to His attributes. True worship places a value on God above all and takes self completely out of the picture. That is the real worship in spirit and truth that God seeks (John 4:23). It is the only true worship that exists in the kingdom of God. No other worship is acceptable to Him.

Are there any ways in which you are simply acknowledging God rather than adoring Him in worship? Are there any temporary things which you are treating as having more worth than God?

Journal closing thoughts and a prayer as you close Day 3.

Day 3 Journal Questions:

What did you experience today as you sought to truly know God?

_____

_____

Did He meet you in a special way?

_____

_____

What did you learn about yourself?
Are you able to say with Job, "my ears had heard of you, but now my eyes have seen you?"

_____

_____

What are the ways in which you were changed by considering His attributes?

_____

_____

Write a brief prayer expressing your heart.

_____

_____

Day 4

A TIME OF JOYFUL SUBMISSION

---—∞∞∞———

I pray that the first three days of your retreat have been refreshing. I also pray that you are feeling rested just from being in the presence of God and away from your normal routine. In the most basic description, that is what the Sabbath is. We have looked back and looked up; it is now time to look ahead.

Focus: Considering the will of God for your life

"Do not conform any longer to the pattern of this world, but be transformed by the renewing of your mind. Then you will be able to test and approve what God's will is—his good, pleasing and perfect will" (Romans 12:2).

"Therefore do not be foolish, but understand what the Lord's will is" (Ephesians 5:17).

Many times, we find ourselves getting bogged down in wondering what the will of God is for our lives. We ask the question with a very specific purpose. We wonder what job God wants us to have or who God wants us to marry. We seek to know God's will for specific circumstances but never get to the point where we realize that He is more concerned with who has control of our will. We can have trouble discerning the will of God if we are not familiar with the various aspects of His will revealed in His Word.

Here, we are considering His revealed moral will: the moral directions and instructions that are found in God's Word. The instructions that are found in Scripture are the expressions of God's desires for our lives. Our free will enables us to disobey those desires and choose what is not good. Our actions and choices have no effect on God's sovereign will, but He does allow us to make choices regarding His moral will. That is a staggering thought.

So many times, God gets the blame for the consequences that come from our choices to disregard His desires. Because of our poor choices, things happen every moment that are outside of the desires that God has revealed for us. Thankfully, because He is ultimately sovereign over everything, God takes each of those instances and uses them to make happen what He wants to accomplish according to His sovereign will.

Our will needs to align with His moral will daily. It is the prayer of Jesus in Luke 22:42, *"Thy will be done."* Praying for God's will to be done is the key for joyful submission. As we begin to truly seek God's will, we are in fact beginning to align our will with His. S. D. Gordon, public speaker and author of the early twentieth century, put it this way:

> "[God's will] is modified by the degree of our consent, and is further modified by the cir-cumstances of our lives. Life has become a badly tangled skein of threads. God with infinite patience and skill is at work untan-gling and bringing the best possible out of the tangle. What is absolutely best is rarely relatively best. That which is best in itself is usually not best under certain circumstances, with human lives in the balance. He could oftentimes do more, and do it in much less time if our human wills were more pliant to

His. He can be trusted. And of course, trust means trust in the darkest dark where you cannot see. And trust means trust. It does not mean test. Where you test you do not trust. Making this our prayer [Thy will be done] means trusting God."[19]

Gordon goes on to say, "Man is the real battlefield. The pitch of the battle is his will. God will not do His will in man without the man's will consenting and Satan cannot."[20]

If you agree with that statement, then you understand that your will is key to God's will being carried out on earth. If you pray for His will to be done and then do not submit your will to His, you are defeating the prayer you are raising and siding with the enemy, giving him control of your will!

If you pray about whether something is God's will when Scripture clearly teaches against it, then you are not in line with His plan for your life. You are living in willful disobedience. You are double-minded, and you have a divided heart. However, if you offer yourself as a living sacrifice and start obediently submitting your will to His in the areas He has revealed, you will find His true and perfect will for your life. Notice that His will is good, pleasing, and perfect. This statement from Paul (Romans 12:1–2) comes following a detailed discussion in the first eleven chapters of Romans of all that God has done. God's will is revealed to all, but those who have come to understand the mercy and grace of God respond to it differently. Obedience to His desires (revealed moral will) flows from a heart that is filled with gratitude and love.

Having spent the last three days first recalibrating yourself, then cleansing yourself, and then basking in who God is, your heart is prepared to hear the gentle promptings of all that He longs to do in this world through your will as it is submitted to His. This is where life gets very exciting as you begin to see yourself as a co-laborer, joyfully submitting to God in full obedience to His will (2 Corinthians 6:1)!

He has chosen to make His appeal to the world through your will submitted to His. In other words, the will of God is allowing you to make real choices through your free will. It is imperative that you get your will aligned with God's in active obedience to those things that you already know are His will as revealed in His Word. In doing so, your mind is transformed, and your actions will begin to follow His leading. Your will has become His will. You have handed over the title and the management of your will to God.

We each have learned practical ways in our daily lives to hand over our will. There are many things that we choose to do during the day that are not necessarily our will but the will of another. Employees submit their will to their employer; children submit their will to their parents. We submit ourselves to a pilot and crew when we board an airplane. Think about all the times that you put aside what you want because somebody else wants something from you.

One simple example is the Global Positioning System (GPS) receiver that many people use to get from one place to the other. It is a satellite-based navigation system made up of a network of twenty-four satellites placed into orbit by the US Department of Defense. GPS satellites circle the earth twice a day in a very precise orbit and transmit information to earth. GPS receivers take this information and use triangulation to calculate the user's exact location.

A GPS receiver must be locked on to the signal of at least three satellites (a trinity of satellites) to calculate a two-dimensional position (latitude and longitude) and track movement. With four or more satellites in view, the receiver can determine the user's three-dimensional position (latitude, longitude, and altitude). Once the user's position has been determined, the GPS unit can calculate other information, such as speed, bearing, track, trip distance, distance to destination, sunrise and sunset times, and more while directing the user to the desired destination.

When you place a GPS unit in your car, you are, in effect, saying that you will submit your will to that device. You program the device to know the destination that you have in mind. You ask the device to chart the course. When that device tells or shows you to turn, you do. If you choose to go a different way, the device recalibrates (and lets you know it needs to) because of your decision to withdraw your submission. How many times have you found yourself reaping the consequences of going the way you wanted instead of the way that the GPS leads? Obviously, there are situations that can cause the GPS to give faulty guidance. At those times, it is important not to submit your will to that imperfect device. God, on the other hand, is never wrong. He never gives faulty guidance. He not only knows your current position, He knows your eternal position and the eternal position of each person ever to have lived and every person yet to live. He has an EPS: Eternal Positioning System.

God the Father, Son, and Holy Spirit have you located every minute of every day. You have been located since before you were born, and you will stay located until the time you breathe your last and beyond (Psalm 139). He has a preferred destination for you, but He allows you, by your will, to choose whether to agree with His preferred destination choice for your life. God is not willing that any should perish (2 Peter 3:8–9). He desires that each person will choose the final destination that He is preparing, but He honors the choice made.

> GOD THE FATHER, SON, AND HOLY SPIRIT HAVE YOU LOCATED EVERY MINUTE OF EVERY DAY.

Once you have come to a point where you have placed all your trust in the work of Jesus Christ alone to secure your salvation, you have entered heaven as the destination on your EPS. You have punched in the coordinates of the room that Jesus has gone to prepare for you (John 14:2). In so doing, you have begun the process of conforming your will to God's. Now it is time to listen and watch the screen of the EPS. It is time to surrender your choice as it relates to the course of your life.

> *"Whether you turn to the right or to the left,*
> *your ears will hear a voice behind you, saying,*
> *'This is the way; walk in it'"* (Isaiah 30:21).

Are you positioned to be ready to hear the directions that God has for your journey? Are you ready to submit to those directions?

I turn the sound off on the GPS receiver in my car. I find the voice to be annoying. Truthfully, many times I feel I have a much better route. By turning off the voice, I do not have to deal with thinking about how I caused the unit to recalibrate according to my choice.

Take a moment and consider the Eternal Positioning System. As a follower of Jesus, you are a person on a journey to your final destination with the Trinity guiding your course. Do you have the volume on? Have you submitted your will to His, or do you regularly withdraw your submission and choose a path of your own? Do you find yourself doubting the direction that He is giving? Do you find yourself ignoring it? Do you find yourself going days without even turning the unit on? Do you turn the volume off?

I want to be careful here. I am not saying that God is standing behind you telling you whether to have ketchup on your French fries. I am saying that God has revealed much information about His moral will in Scripture. The way to turn on the EPS unit is to spend time in His Word. He has revealed His will in the Bible. It is there you will find what He desires for your life. You need to be reading Scripture and allowing Scripture to read you to make wise choices and do the moral will of God.

If you can learn to obey the moral will of God as revealed in Scripture, your choices will be aligned with His for your life. This obedience flows from gratitude and love. Many people are trying to determine God's will for their life in a certain situation, yet they stand in willful disobedience to God's moral will that has been revealed. What makes that person believe they would follow the will of God for the specific situation at hand? What makes them think that God would reveal it? They have not learned how to follow the will of God in other areas of life. Instead, they are setting their own course; thus, God will allow them to do so even when it brings pain.

Today, we will look at some passages where God makes His moral will for your life known. It is important that you ask yourself if you are on the right course. It is also important to ask yourself if you even want to be on the right course. Ask yourself the following questions today:

How would your life change if your will was fully aligned with God's?

How would your family's life change?

How would the world change?

_____

_____

_____

Look up the following passages and consider the questions.

John 4:34
How can doing the will of God be nourishment for your soul? Have you ever considered it in those terms before?

_____

_____

_____

_____

_____

Deuteronomy 6:4–9; Psalms 37:30–31; 40:4–8;
119:9–11, 97–105
There are many verses about the law of the Lord being
written on the heart. What does it mean for the law of the
Lord to be written on your heart? How would that help you
desire to do God's will?

_____

_____

_____

_____

_____

_____

_____

Ephesians 5:17; Colossians 1:9–10
What is the difference between knowing the will of God
and understanding the will of God? How does the difference impact the way you follow God?

_____

---

1 Thessalonians 4:3–7; 2 Peter 3:14
God's will is that you be holy (sanctified in the NIV). When you consider all the times that you have wondered about what the will of God is for your life, have you ever considered that it could be summed up in the following sentence? *"God's will is for you to be holy"* (1 Thessalonians 4:3, NLT). How do you respond to this statement? What are ways that you can move toward holiness? What stops you from moving toward holiness? What level of sin are you comfortable with in your life?

Luke 9:21–27
God's will requires that you deny yourself, which is not at all easy. All of us have become quite comfortable with getting our own desires. Sacrifice is not a common word, and many times what we call sacrifice is taken from the excess, without any pain. God's will for your life includes resurrection. It is very easy to get excited about the coming

resurrection, but this passage along with Romans 6:5–7, Galatians 2:20, and Philippians 3:10–11 make it clear that crucifixion must come into a life before there can be a resurrection. God's will is the death of your sinful desires. Those must be taken to the cross. Are there any areas of your life that you need to deny? Have you been crucified with Christ?

_____

_____

_____

_____

_____

2 Peter 3:9

_____

_____

_____

_____

_____

Ephesians 4 and 5
Take some time to read through Ephesians 4 and 5. What part of God's will for your life is He revealing for you to experience right now?

_____

_____

_____

_____

_____

Read the following prayer that was penned by Jonathan Edwards, the great American theologian of the eighteenth century, in his diary at the age of nineteen. Is this a prayer that you are willing to offer as you seek the will of God for your life?

"I have been before God; and have given myself, all that I am and have to God, so that I am not in any respect my own: I can claim no right in myself, no right in this understanding, this will, these affections that are in me; neither have I any right to this body, or any of its members: No right to this tongue, these hands, nor feet: No right to these senses, these eyes, these ears, this smell or this taste. *I have given myself clear away,* and have not retained anything as my own. I have been to God this morning and told him that I gave myself wholly to him. . . . I have this morning told him, that I did take him for my whole portion and felicity [contentment], looking on nothing else as any part of my happiness, nor acting as if it were; and his law for the constant rule of my obedience; and would fight with all my might against the world, the flesh, and the devil, to the end of my life. And did believe in Jesus Christ, and receive him as a prince and a saviour; and would adhere to the faith and obedience of the gospel, how hazardous and difficult soever the profession and practice of it may be. That I did receive the blessed Spirit as my teacher, sanctifier, and only comforter; and cherish all his motions to enlighten, purify, confirm, comfort, and assist me. *This I have done.* And I pray God, for the sake of Christ, to look upon it as a self-dedication; and to receive me now as entirely his own, and deal with me in all respects as such; whether he afflicts me or prospers me, or whatever he pleases to do with me, who am his."[21]

This prayer is a reminder that the will of God is dynamic. Much the same as the GPS, God reveals His will to you as you go along the journey. He has an active involvement in your life (Isaiah 48:17). Your goal must be to follow His directions as they unfold before you. He is not so concerned with exactly what you are doing; He is more concerned with who you are while you are doing it.

So how should you go about seeking God for special guidance? It is important if you are a committed follower of Christ, that you are actively obeying His revealed desires for you, and that you are willing to obey whatever He asks. The late Paul Little, former worker at InterVarsity Christian Fellowship and associate professor of evangelism at Trinity Evangelical Divinity School, makes that point clear in his booklet *Affirming the Will of God*. He goes on to reveal there are four checkpoints that you can use to affirm God's will for your life.

1. The principles taught in the Word of God are the foundational base for determining God's will.
2. God guides and directs through circumstances. Situations in your life can be God's hand leading you. Care is needed here to assure that decisions are not made solely on circumstance.
3. God guides through the counsel of other Christians. When seeking the advice of another Christian, make sure the person you are talking to is a fully committed, genuine follower of Christ.

4. God Himself will confirm His will as you diligently bring your petitions before Him. You must spend time with God if you are to discern His direction.[22]

Are there specific things that God revealed to you today about your will?

_____

_____

Are there special things that He has revealed about His will?

_____

_____

Have you seen the importance of spending time in His presence and in His Word in order to know His will?

_____

_____

Journal closing thoughts and a prayer as you conclude Day 4.

Day 4 Journal Questions:

What did you experience today as you sought to discover if you truly are submitted to God?

_____

_____

Did He meet you in a special way? How?

_____

_____

What did you learn about yourself?

_____

_____

In what ways has your understanding of God's will for your life changed?

_____

_____

What are some specific areas that will change for you going forward?

_____

_____

Write a brief prayer expressing your heart.

_____

_____

Postlude

A TIME TO RE-ENTER

———∞∞∞———

You may assume that once you return from your retreat, the experience is over. Not true! Your return is the beginning of an inevitable transition: merging your new experience into your old life. You have spent some very special days focused narrowly on the person of God and His touch in your life without the distractions that can normally interfere. It is probably safe to assume that you were introduced to new things in your relationship with God, new ways of hearing His voice, and new ways of experiencing an abundantly free life. You will more than likely mourn at not being able to maintain a relationship with God at this level once you return to your daily life. It is important that you are very intentional going forward.

Each of the four previous days you were asked to write a prayer. I recommend that you rewrite those prayers on one piece of paper. Begin to use that as a prayer document for yourself and begin to take those action steps in the strength that you have been given in Christ! In his book *The Great Omission*, Dallas Willard writes this:

> "Sabbath is a way of life (Hebrews 4:3, 9–11). It sets us free from bondage to our own efforts. Only in this way can we come to the power and joy of a radiant life in ministry and work, a blessing to all we touch. And yet Sabbath is almost totally absent from the

existence of contemporary Christians and their ministers."[23]

The first time that Sabbath is mentioned in Scripture is Exodus 16. Take a moment and look at verses 23–36. Notice first that the Sabbath is to the LORD. Notice second that it is given as a gift to the Israelites who have been in the bondage of slavery for 400 years without a rest period. Look carefully at verse 30: "So the people rested on the seventh day."

God has designed the Sabbath for you and for Himself. You have had a small taste of the design He has for your life. I am sure that you have found at least some moments in

YOU HAVE NOT FELT THE NEED TO PERFORM FOR HIM BUT THE NEED TO JUST BE WITH HIM.

which you have found your joy in the LORD. You have not felt the need to perform for Him but the need to just be with Him. Remember what He said about that need to Martha when she came to ask him about Mary in Luke 10:41–42? We have lost the value of simply sitting at the feet of Jesus as we have allowed ourselves to fall into the bondage of slavery in this world of busyness and instant self-gratification. We have scheduled the Sabbath out of our lives and in the process have taken the holy day—the sanctuary in time—that God set apart for Himself and used it for our pleasure and purposes. Doing so comes with a price. We attempt to find our joy in performance, leisure, work, or one of a hundred other areas and thereby miss finding our joy in the LORD. I would suggest that we live in willful disobedience regarding the Sabbath.

In this retreat, I pray that you have tasted the relief that God longs to give you in time set apart and made holy just for Him. You have felt the joy that overwhelms you as you set this time aside. I submit that God has designed for you to experience this relief, rest, and joy weekly.

Consider the following questions:

Is it possible for you to experience something like this each week?

_____

_____

Where can you find a time in your week to set aside time for God? What would that look like for you?

_____

_____

Do you see now how essential this time is? Do you believe you can ignore the need for time with God?

_____

_____

Remember that if you choose to enter this wonderful world of Sabbath, it is choosing to open the gift of a special time set aside for you and God to walk in the garden in the cool of the day. It is rest from all that would overtake you. It is a time to try as hard as possible to leave the cares of the world behind and focus on the eternal nature of your very soul. Sabbath awakens and empowers the eternal perspective that you were designed to embrace. In the process of this special time with God, the sufferings of this world fall away as light and momentary (2 Corinthians 4:16–5:20). Consider the Sabbath. Make it holy in your life. Make it an anticipated time with God. Put off all the excuses that may be keeping you from this special time and choose that which is better time at the feet of Jesus.

How is the Sabbath viewed in your life and in your environment?

_____

_____

What do your friends think of when you speak about the Sabbath? Is it an exciting topic of conversation? How is it viewed in your church? In your workplace?

_____

_____

How could observing the Sabbath bring your family together in intimacy with God?

_____

_____

The late Abraham Joshua Heschel was a Polish-born American rabbi and one of the leading Jewish theologians and Jewish philosophers of the 20th century. In the introduction to his book *The Sabbath*, his daughter, Susannah Heschel, gives a special insight into the excitement Sabbath participation brings to a Jewish home.

> "When my father raised his Kiddush cup on
> Friday evenings, closed his eyes and chanted
> the prayer sanctifying the wine, I always felt
> a rush of emotion. As he chanted with an old,

sacred family melody, he blessed the wine and the Sabbath with his prayer, and I also felt he was blessing my life and that of everyone at the table. I treasured those moments.

Friday evenings in my home were the climax of the week, as they are for every religious Jewish family. My mother and I kindled the lights for the Sabbath, and all of a sudden I felt transformed, emotionally and even physically. After lighting the candles in the dining room, we would walk into the living room, which had windows overlooking the Hudson River, facing west, and we would marvel at the sunset that soon arrived.

The sense of peace that came upon us as we kindled the lights was created, in part, by the hectic tension of Fridays. Preparation for a holy day, my father often said, was as important as the day itself. During the busy mornings my mother shopped for groceries, and in the afternoons the atmosphere grew increasingly nervous as she cooked. My father came home from his office an hour or two before sunset to take care of his own preparations, and as the last minutes of the workweek came to a close, both of my parents were in the kitchen, frantically trying to remember what they might have forgotten to prepare— Had the kettle boiled? Was the blech covering the stove? Was the oven turned on?

Then, suddenly, it was time: twenty minutes before sunset. Whatever hadn't been finished in the kitchen we simply left behind as

we lit the candles and blessed the arrival of
the Sabbath. My father writes, "The Sabbath
comes like a caress, wiping away fear, sorrow
and somber memories."[24]

What stirs in your heart as you read this insight? Is there
a longing for this type of anticipation for the Sabbath?
Consider what the Sabbath is in your life and in the life of
your family and how it brings anticipation. What comes
like a caress to those you love the most? What wipes away
your fear and sorrows?

_____

_____

_____

_____

_____

I am not suggesting you must start with a twenty-four-
hour block of time. What I am encouraging is an extended
time, sacrificially set aside, to reflect upon and review your
relationship with God. I am talking about a *sanctuary in
time*—a special place in time where you go regularly to worship God. It is a time that you have consecrated for Him. It is
a time to look ahead to who you may become as you allow
special time with Him to shape and transform you into the
peace-filled child He has intended for you to be. It is a time
to rest and reflect.

Too many times we can fall into the rut of doing the
things we think we must do. Creating space for rest in your
life will require some tough decisions. You will need to say
no to some expectations. You will need to prioritize that

which supplies your life with true significance and meaning. You will need to place a high value on being with God for His sake—and for yours. Seek Him in this. Carefully and prayerfully determine what Sabbath looks like for you with your Father. Design the time to fit how you can best find yourself in His presence. It may mean that you are outside. It may mean you are inside. It may be that you curl up with the Bible or another book.

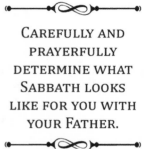

CAREFULLY AND PRAYERFULLY DETERMINE WHAT SABBATH LOOKS LIKE FOR YOU WITH YOUR FATHER.

It may mean that you walk and talk with others about the things of God. It may be that you are just quiet before Him. It may mean a long, quiet walk. It may mean a walk filled with song and prayers that you lift to Him. You may just find yourself talking His ear off!

You may find your time spent with a good friend in God's presence, not saying anything to each other, but both in communication with the Almighty, coming together at the end of the day to share what the day was like for each of you. You may find yourself embracing special time with your family considering the awesomeness of God in your relationships with each other. You may find joy in understanding leisure in a new way. God is longing for you to stop and take the gift of Sabbath that He is offering to you. He is waiting for you to stop so you can find your joy in Him.

Take the time today to think about the amount and quality of time that you spend developing intimacy with God. Try to lay the groundwork for what a regular Sabbath experience may look like for you and your family. Take the time to design Sabbath into your week.

WEEKLY SABBATH PLAN

—⚬◦⚬—

Y our retreat experience has followed a set pattern for time with God. If you have experienced this, you know that it took a few hours or perhaps days to get to a point where you were ready to really hear God's voice. If you choose to have a weekly Sabbath time with God, you will find that it does not take long to find yourself in His presence in this special way because you will not have wandered far from it. I suggest a possible weekly Sabbath quiet time experience that would include each of the four steps used on the retreat week. You and God can determine the amount of time spent in each step.

1. Check for joy robbers. It is very important to start your Sabbath time by checking your heart to see if anything has robbed your joy. Has anything come into your life that has caused you to doubt the pleasure that God has in you or the pleasure that you have been designed to have in Him?

2. Cleanse your heart. It is very hard to sit in the presence of God with unconfessed sin in your life. Reflect. Consider if you have been proud in any way. Are there ways that you have relied upon your own initiatives in self-sufficiency? Pray the prayer of Psalm 139:23–24. Ask God to search you and to reveal what He has found.

3. Focus on God's attributes and majesty. Read the psalms for this purpose. Consider the awesomeness and majesty of God. Remind yourself often of how

much peace you can embrace because of the faithfulness and unchanging nature of your God.

4. Seek Him for His will. Only God knows what the next week holds for you. Only God knows what is coming. He is the One who is sovereign over it, and He is the One who can prepare you for what lies ahead. It is critical to keep your will in touch with God's. Find the desire to follow what He has for you. Align your will with His. When the church was in its infancy, Gamaliel was used by God to offer a great prophecy: *"For if their purpose or activity is of human origin, it will fail. But if it is from God, you will not be able to stop these men; you will only find yourselves fighting God"* (Acts 5:38–39).

You have the opportunity each week to choose. You can do what you think is best from what you have determined on your own or go to the almighty, all-knowing God and find His good, pleasing, and perfect will for your life.

You will find the Sabbath to be a great time to seek God for what He may have for you in the week ahead. Mark 1:35–39 reveals Jesus setting that example for us. This does not mean that you will get clear direction for every possible thing that will come up. Rather, seeking God in this way aligns your heart with His so that you can hear His voice as He directs you (Isaiah 30:21).

In each of these steps, value solitude and silence with your Lord more than anything. Value quietness in His presence—even for a short time. As you get a rhythm in place in your life for Sabbath, you will find favorite authors, favorite spots, and favorite ways to spend time with God. It is well worth the effort to anticipate the day and prepare to be with Him.

PRINCIPLES
OF THE SABBATH

———∞———

These are extra thoughts about some of the basic principles of the Sabbath. They can be used in the evening or any other time and can be useful for group discussion.

Principle of the Sabbath #1

The Sabbath is a place to consider the balance of your life. Richard Swenson, a physician-researcher, best-selling author, and award-winning educator, has a helpful way of looking at this:

Power – Load = Margin

Power is made up of factors such as energy, skills, time, training, emotional and physical strength, faith, finances, and social supports.

Load is made up of such factors as work, problems, obligations and commitments, expectations (internal and external), debt, deadlines, and interpersonal conflicts.

When our load is greater than our power, we enter into negative margin status—that is, we are overloaded.

Endured long term, this is not a healthy state. Severe negative margin for an extended period of time is another name for burnout.[25]

Intentionality is the key to keeping this equation in balance.

Steps to creating and protecting margin

1) Discover your power level.
How has God equipped you (Deuteronomy 8:17–18)?

_____

_____

What power do you have? What are the limits of
your power?

_____

_____

How has this changed over the seasons of your life?

_____

_____

2) Discover your load.
What are the items that make up your load?

_____

_____

Who contributes to your load?

_____

_____

3) Determine what is important.
What load has God designed to be taken from your power?

_____

_____

Seek and follow God's plan for your life; see Mark 1:35–38 and John 11:5–6.

What is your mission statement? Having a personal and family mission statement allows you to say "yes" to the right things. See Acts 20:24.

_____

_____

What is your priority when it comes to load?

_____

_____

Are you an impulse spender of power? Do you allow others to draw inappropriately from your power?

_____

_____

4) Budget margin into your life. Intentionality requires that you set goals.
Make a calendar that shows where you spend your power Budget time for margin into your schedule.

5) Evaluate

Rest is needed (Mark 6:31). Regularly set time to review-Sabbath rest.

Get together with God—are you completing the work He has given you (Colossians 4:17)?

In other words, are you carrying the right load (Matthew 11:28–30) ?

_____

_____

As you begin to consider entering an extended time with God, think about this equation and determine where you are out of balance. More than likely, that is what is keeping you from Sabbath.

Principle of the Sabbath # 2

The Sabbath is a place to find rest: "Come with me by yourselves to a quiet place and get some rest" (Mark 6:31b).

This is a powerful verse that will prepare your heart for the retreat time. Think carefully about each of the sections of this verse:

1) Come with me
"I am the way, the truth and the life" (John 14:6).

How many times do you ask Jesus to come with you instead of seeking to go with Him? How can you learn to go with Jesus?

_____

_____

2) by yourselves
"Sit here while I go over there and pray" (Matthew 26:36).

How do you anticipate spending time with God by yourself?

_____

_____

3) to a quiet place
"Be still and know that I am God" (Psalm 46:10).

How difficult is it for you to find a quiet place?

_____

_____

4) and get some rest
"Come to me, all you who are weary and burdened, and I will give you rest" (Matthew 11:28).

Do you find yourself weary? What would it be like to find true rest?

_____

_____

Principle of the Sabbath #3: Silence and Solitude
Read Kings 18:45-19:18

The Sabbath is a place to practice silence and solitude.

Silence and solitude are missing elements from our society. They are elusive and unknown to most. Because of the fast-paced world that we live in, we can miss time alone with God. We crave noise and distraction, even though it is not what we have been designed for. Is it possible we fear the silence?

How would you describe solitude?

_____

_____

_____

_____

_____

_____

"Solitude is the furnace of transformation. . . . [It] is the place of the great struggle and the great encounter—the struggle against the compulsions of the false self, and the encounter with the loving God who offers himself as the substance of the new self"[26] (Henri Nouwen).

How would you describe silence?

_____

_____

_____

_____

_____

_____

"Silence helps us drop beneath the superficiality of our mental constructs to the place of the heart that is deeper in its reality than anything the mind can capture or express in words. It is the place of longing and desire and reaching for that which we do not yet have. In this wordless place the whole of our person turns itself toward God and waits to be addressed by God"[27] (Ruth Haley Barton).

Consider Elijah and his relationship with God in this passage:

This is a great account of the sovereign power of God. He held Satan back from being able to bring fire to the sacrifice and showed the splendor of His might. Elijah was blessed to be the one chosen by God to represent Him. Great battles bring great weariness. It is far more dangerous to come down from a mountain than it is to ascend. God knows that, and He knows that times of weariness need a special touch from Him. He also knows that weariness can cause you to lose proper perspective. That is what happened to Elijah.

God took this great prophet and allowed him to rest, brought him nourishment and then asked the great question. God asked Elijah the question, "What are you doing here?" Notice that Elijah had a rehearsed answer. He repeats the answer twice. When you feel overwhelmed, you can fall into the trap of living in a rehearsed pain that is not true. You need to hear the voice of God to speak truth into your life.

Is God asking you the same question? Has anything brought doubt into your mind?

_____

_____

God tells Elijah to listen for His voice. The voice comes in silence and solitude as God whispers softly the truths that Elijah needed to hear.

Can you identify any noises and distractions that are keeping you from hearing truth?

_____

_____

How do the noises keep you from hearing the questions that God is asking of you?

_____

_____

How can you prepare yourself to hear the whisper of God?

_____

_____

Principle of the Sabbath #4

The Sabbath brings God pleasure. Read Genesis 2:3.

God longs to spend quality time with His created ones. You have been created from relationship for relationship. Many times the Sabbath is viewed as a time for us to get rest; therefore, the rationalization is made that if rest is not needed, the Sabbath can be ignored. Sabbath brings pleasure to God if observed from a pure heart (Isaiah 1:1–15). He loves to be with His children, especially when they have chosen to actively be with Him!

Ultimately, being with Him in relationship is your purpose in life! Bringing glory to God is best accomplished as you live your life considering what will bring Him pleasure and then living that out.

How does observing the Sabbath bring God pleasure?

_____

_____

What difference does it make to consider the Sabbath in this way?

_____

_____

How much pleasure is the LORD deriving from your life? How much time in your life do you spend considering how you can bring God pleasure?

Principle of the Sabbath #5

The Sabbath celebrates deliverance. Read Deuteronomy 5:12–15.

The Sabbath brings great pleasure to God when we take the time to remember the bondage from which we have been delivered. It is very interesting to think that God would go to such lengths to describe the reason for and extent of the Sabbath within the Ten Commandments. Reflecting on the deliverance you have received gives you the assurance that He is faithful to deliver you from the other things in your life that hold you captive. It is so important for you to regularly remember the freedom from bondage that is available to you.

Have you noticed that as you reflect on the items in your life that need repentance that you feel great deliverance when you choose to receive His forgiveness?

_____

_____

From what have you been delivered?

_____

_____

What is there that is still holding you captive?

_____

_____

How can Sabbath help you celebrate deliverance from that captivity?

_____

_____

Principle of the Sabbath #6

The Sabbath is a gift. Read Exodus 16:29 and Mark 2:23–28.

The Sabbath is not an obligation or requirement, although at one time it was considered as such and still can be today. When time is spent with God as an obligation or requirement, there is a real chance that the joy will be missed, which is not at all what God intended. It is important to remember that God has created the Sabbath as a gift. Because it is a gift, you have the choice to leave it unopened. There is much written and spoken about when it comes to the Sabbath.

IT IS IMPORTANT TO REMEMBER THAT GOD HAS CREATED THE SABBATH AS A GIFT.

Many feel there are good reasons to consider that we are no longer obligated to keep the Sabbath and so encourage believers to put the Sabbath aside.

Yet there are no good reasons that I have heard or read for not opening the gift of regular, special time spent with the Lover of your soul. Should you choose to keep the Sabbath out of obligation or choose not to observe it because you believe it is no longer required, you will miss opening and enjoying the joyous gift that God has designed as part of Sabbath rest in Him.

In what ways do you view the Sabbath as an obligation?

_____

_____

In what ways do you view the Sabbath as a gift?

_____

_____

How does your view of the Sabbath affect the way you enter that time with God?

_____

_____

Principle of the Sabbath #7

The Sabbath puts His work ahead of mine. Read Genesis 1:31 and Psalm 19:1–4.

Taking the time to consider God's attributes and His handiwork impacts your view of Him tremendously. If God took the time to pause and consider His handiwork, how much more important is it for you to do the same? It is very easy in the busyness of life to miss the incredible handiwork of the Master Creator. Focusing carefully on what He has made causes you to celebrate Him in a special way.

What do you think of as outstanding when you think about God's work?

_____

_____

_____

_____

_____

_____

_____

What things keep you from putting God's work ahead of your own?

_____

_____

Principle of the Sabbath #8

The Sabbath is a time to cease. Read Exodus 16:21–30.

The Sabbath is a time to stop gathering and collecting. This is a very hard teaching and very difficult to put into practice. It really becomes a question of trust. Do you trust that God is able to supply all that you need if you set aside time to be with Him? This account of the manna reveals that some of the Israelites were not able to stop accumulating that one day of the week. We are not all that different from the Israelites. We have a very hard time ceasing our endless activities.

What are the things that keep you from a time of ceasing?

_____

_____

What would it look like for you to have one day a week that you did not purchase something?

_____

_____

What if you stopped accumulating?

_____

_____

_____

_____

_____

How does your inability to cease reveal a lack of trust in the provision of God?

_____

_____

Principle of the Sabbath #9

The Sabbath is a time for rest beyond leisure. Read Ecclesiastes 2:1–3 and Isaiah 58:13–14.

The Sabbath is not a pursuit of leisure. It is a pursuit of joy. Our purpose is to pursue God, but some have tried to pursue pleasure as the purpose for life. Pursuing leisure has become an addiction for people. People strive to make enough to play hard and then justify playing hard because they worked so hard to get the stuff to play with.

It is a vicious cycle and a never-ending trap that spirals a person away from God into the snare that the enemy has set for them. What a contrast to what God has designed in the Sabbath! The Sabbath allows rest beyond leisure free of charge. There is no cost of admission, and there is no waiting in line! It is true rest.

God longs for you to have leisure time, and leisure is a part of the Sabbath experience. The danger comes when leisure becomes the focus of the time set aside, and God is not the central focus. That is not Sabbath.

After a day of leisure, how many times have you been more tired than when you in the day started?

_____

_____

How have you viewed Sabbath as a great time to take part in excessive leisure? According to Mark Buchanan, writer and professor, in his book *The Rest Of God*:

> "One of the largest obstacles to true Sabbath-keeping is leisure. Leisure is what Sabbath becomes when we no longer know how to sanctify time. Leisure is Sabbath bereft of the sacred. It is a vacation—literally, a vacating, an evacuation."[28]

PRINCIPLES OF THE SABBATH

How has leisure become vacating in your life?

_____

_____

Principle of the Sabbath #10

The Sabbath is a time to control yourself. Read Genesis 2:2–3 and Galatians 5:22–23.

The last of the principles to be considered is that of self-control. Self-control is contained within the fruit of the Spirit in the life of a follower of Jesus. Self-control is within the nature and character of God.

Stop and consider God ceasing from creating. Imagine all that God could have continued to create if He hadn't stopped! God is limitless in all His thoughts and ways—and yet He chose self-control. In so doing, He left an example for His creation to follow. Proverbs 25:28 tells us, *"Like a city whose walls are broken down is a man who lacks self-control."*

Consider your life and how you exhibit self-control. Can you see that ceasing for Sabbath really does require that you control yourself? Of course, as you align with Spirit this becomes the self-control of God revealing itself through you.

Do you ever feel as though your city walls are broken down? Can you see areas where you lack self-control?

How can Sabbath help you bring self-control into your life?

_____

_____

THREE-DAY SABBATH RETREAT PLAN

I t may be that you are unable to get away for a full week, but you would like to use the material in this book for an abbreviated retreat. The following guide may be helpful for you.

Evening prior: Read over the Sabbath Eve chapter and look at the first Sabbath principle.

Day One:

Morning: Day One in guidebook. If you are with a group, come together for lunch and talk about the things you discovered that were robbing your joy. If time allows, you can consider some of the principles of the Sabbath.

Afternoon: Day Two in the guidebook. If you are in a group, come back together for dinner and then have conversation about how God spoke into your life about confession. Look at some more of the principles of the Sabbath as time allows.

Day Two:

Morning: Day Three in the guidebook. Come together for lunch and then talk about your morning praising God for His majesty. Consider a couple more principles of the Sabbath.

Afternoon: Day Four in the guidebook. Come back together for dinner and then have conversation about

God's will for your life. Look over any remaining principles of the Sabbath.

Day Three:

Morning: Consider the Postlude in the guidebook. Spend time seeking God for how to have Sabbath become a valued part of your regular routine.

BIBLIOGRAPHY

―――∞∞∞―――

O n the following pages are some of the books and
authors that have been important to me in the journey
of discovering all that God has designed me to be. God has
used various parts of each of these books to continue to
shape my heart and mind, and for that I am grateful. Many
of them have been very instrumental in my understanding
of how to have the Sabbath be part of my regular experience.
If you choose to read any of the titles, you may find where
the thoughts of the author impacted me, and you may find
new and exciting ways that God will impact you.

Enjoy.

Allendar, Dan B. *Sabbath* (Nashville: Thomas
Nelson, 2009).

Anderson, James. *For God's Sake, Rest* (Pleasant
Word, 2007).

Anderson, Neil. *Victory Over the Darkness: Realizing the
Power of Your Identity in Christ* (Ventura: Regal, 1990).

Barber, Cyril J. *Nehemiah and the Dynamics of Effective
Leadership* (Neptune, New Jersey: Loizeaux Bothers, 1976).

Barclay, William. *The Gospel of Luke: The New Daily Study
Bible* (Westminster: John Knox Press; Revised, Updated edition 2001).

Barton, Ruth Haley. *Invitation to Solitude and Silence*
(Downers Grove: InterVarsity Press, 2010).

Buchanan, Mark. *The Rest of God: Restoring Your Soul by
Restoring Sabbath* (Nashville: W Publishing Group, 2006).

Curtis, Brent & Eldredge, John. *The Sacred Romance* (Nashville: Thomas Nelson, 1997).

DeMoss, Nancy Leigh. *Brokenness: The Heart God Revives* (Chicago: Moody Press, 2002).

DeMoss, Nancy Leigh. *Choosing Forgiveness: Your Journey to Freedom* (Chicago: Moody Press, 2006).

DeMoss, Nancy Leigh. *Holiness: The Heart God Purifies* (Chicago: Moody Press, 2005).

DeMoss, Nancy Leigh. *Surrender: The Heart God Controls* (Chicago: Moody Press, 2005).

DeMoss, Nancy Leigh & Grissom, Tim. *Seeking Him: Experiencing the Joy of*
Personal Revival (Chicago: Moody Publishers, 2004).

Edman, V. Raymond. *They Found the Secret* (Grand Rapids: Zondervan, 1984).

Edwards, Jonathan. *The Works of President Edwards Vol. 1* (Worcester: Isaiah Thomas, 1808).

Eldredge, John. *The Journey of Desire* (Nashville: Thomas Nelson, 2000).

Foster, Richard. *Celebration of Discipline* (San Francisco: Harper Collins, 1998).

Gordon, S. D. *Quiet Talks on Prayer* (New York: Fleming H. Revell Company, 1904).

Hansen, David. *Long Wandering Prayer* (Downers Grove: InterVarsity Press, 2001).

Heschel, Abraham Joshua. *The Sabbath: Its Meaning for Modern Man* (New York:
Noonday, 2005).

Hession, Roy. *The Calvary Road* (CLC Ministries, 1980).

Hollingsworth, Amy. *The Simple Faith of Mister Rogers* (Nashville: Integrity, 2005).

Hummel, Charles E. *Tyranny of the Urgent* (Downers Grove: InterVarsity Press, 1994).

Ingram, Chip. *God: As He Longs For You To See Him* (Grand Rapids: Baker Books, 2004).

Keller, Phillip. *A Shepherd Looks at Psalm 23* (Grand Rapids: Zondervan, 1970).

Kent, Keri Wyatt. *Rest: Living in Sabbath Simplicity* (Grand Rapids: Zondervan, 2009).

Kraft, Alan. *Good News For Those Trying Harder* (Colorado Springs: David C. Cook, 2008).

Lewis, C.S. *The Weight of Glory* (New York: HarperOne; HarperCollins REV ed. Edition, March 2001).

Little, Paul E. *Affirming the Will of God* (Downers Grove: InterVarsity Press, 2001).

Munger, Robert Boyd. *My Heart-Christ's Home* (Downer's Grove: InterVarsity Press, 1986).

Muyskens, Nancy Stark. *The Curtain Is Torn* (Xulon Press, 2006).

Nouwen, Henri. *Making All Things New: An Invitation to the Spiritual Life* (HarperSanFrancisco 1981).

Nouwen, Henri. *In the Name of Jesus* (New York: Crossroad, 2001).

Nouwen, Henri. *The Way of the Heart* (New York: Ballantine Books, 2003).

Owens, Buddy. *The Way of a Worshipper* (Lake Forest, CA: Purpose Driven Publishing, 2004).

Packer, J. I. *Knowing God* (Downer's Grove: InterVarsity Press, 1993).

Patterson, Ben. *The Grand Essentials* (Waco: Word, 1987).

Pink, Arthur W. *The Attributes of God* (Grand Rapids: Baker Books, 1975).

Piper, John. *The Dangerous Duty of Delight* (Colorado Springs: Multnomah Books, 2001).

Scazzero, Peter. *The Emotionally Healthy Church* (Grand Rapids: Zondervan, 2003).

Simpson, Albert B. (1891) *Himself* Retrieved from https://www.biblebelievers.com/simpson-ab_himself.html.

Sleeth, Matthew M.D. *24/6: A Prescription for a Healthier, Happier Life* (Carol Stream, IL: Tyndale House Publishers, Inc. 2012).

Smith, Christian and Denton Melina Lundquist. *Soul Searching: The Religious and Spiritual Lives of American Teenagers,* (Oxford University Press; Reprint edition, April 13, 2009).

Stowell, Joseph M. *Following Christ* (Grand Rapids: Zondervan, 1996).

Stowell, Joseph M. *Loving Christ: Recapturing Your Passion For Jesus* (Grand Rapids: Zondervan, 2000).

Swenson, Richard A. *Margin: Restoring Emotional, Physical, Financial, and Time Reserves to Overloaded Lives (*NavPress, 2004).

Swindoll, Charles R. *Laugh Again: Experience Outrageous Joy* (Dallas: Word, 1992).

Tozer, A.W. *The Knowledge of the Holy* (San Francisco: HarperCollins, 1961).

Willard, Dallas. *The Great Omission* (New York: HarperOne; Reprint edition, May 13, 2014).

Endnotes

Title Page
1   Anderson, James. *For God's Sake, Rest* (Pleasant Word, 2007) page 24.

Introduction Page
2   Simpson, Albert B. (1891) *Himself* Retrieved from https://www.biblebelievers.com/simpson-ab_himself.html.

Sabbath Retreat Eve
3   Heschel, Abraham Joshua. The Sabbath, Its Meaning for Modern Man (New York: Noonday, 2005) page 9.

4   Anderson, James. *For God's Sake, Rest* (Pleasant Word, 2007) page 53.

5   Nouwen, Henri. *Making All Things New: An Invitation to the Spiritual Life* (HarperSanFrancisco 1981) page 69.

Day One
6   Augustine of Hippo, Confessions.

7   Lewis, C.S. *The Weight of Glory* (New York: HarperOne; HarperCollins REV ed. Edition, March 2001) page 26.

8   Barber, Cyril J. *Nehemiah and the Dynamics of Effective Leadership* (Neptune, New Jersey: Loizeaux Bothers, 1976) page 22.

9   Foster, Richard. *Celebration of Discipline* (San Francisco: Harper Collins, 1998) page 96.

Day Two

10 Barclay, William. *The Gospel of Luke: The New Daily Study Bible* (Westminster: John Knox Press; Revised, Updated edition 2001) page 114.

11 Hession, Roy. *The Calvary Road* (CLC Ministries, 1980) page 21.

12 Anderson, James. *For God's Sake, Rest* (Pleasant Word, 2007) page 94.

13 Peacock, Charlie. (1991). In The Light. On *Love Life* [Cassette Tape]. Sparrow Records (1991).

14 Kraft, Alan. *Good News For Those Trying Harder* (Colorado Springs: David C. Cook, 2008) pages 45–47.

Day Three

15 Tozer, A.W. *The Knowledge of the Holy* (San Francisco: HarperCollins, 1961) page 1.

16 Smith, Christian and Denton Melina Lundquist. *Soul Searching: The Religious and Spiritual Lives of American Teenagers,* (Oxford University Press; Reprint edition, April 13, 2009).

17 Nouwen, Henri. *In the Name of Jesus* (New York: Crossroad, 2001) page 30.

18 Hansen, David. *Long Wandering Prayer* (Downers Grove: InterVarsity Press, 2001) page 37.

Day Four

19 Gordon, S. D. *Quiet Talks on Prayer* (New York: Fleming H. Revell Company, 1904) page 60.

20 Ibid., page 64.

21 Edwards, Jonathan. *The Works of President Edwards Vol. 1* (Worcester: Isaiah Thomas,1808) pages 19–20.

22 Little, Paul E. *Affirming the Will of God* (Downers Grove: InterVarsity Press, 2001).

23 Willard, Dallas. *The Great Omission* (New York: HarperOne; Reprint edition, May 13, 2014) pages 34–35.

24 Heschel, Abraham Joshua. *The Sabbath, Its Meaning for Modern Man* (New York: Noonday, 2005) page vii-viii.

Principles of the Sabbath
25 Swenson, Richard A. *Margin: Restoring Emotional, Physical, Financial, and Time Reserves to Overloaded Lives* (NavPress, 2004) The equation shown is taken from the principles in the book.

26 Nouwen, Henri. *The Way of the Heart* (New York: Ballantine Books, 2003) pages 15–16.

27 Barton, Ruth Haley. *Invitation to Solitude and Silence* (Downers Grove: InterVarsity Press, 2010) Page 74.

28 Buchanan, Mark. *The Rest of God: Restoring Your Soul by Restoring Sabbath* (Nashville: W Publishing Group, 2006) page 35.

CPSIA information can be obtained
at www.ICGtesting.com
Printed in the USA
JSHW022304210722
28339JS00001B/9